Archie Bowman

Be a philosopher; but, amidst all your philosophy, be still a man.
    David Hume, *An Enquiry Concerning Human Understanding*

Archie Bowman

Foot Soldier, German PoW and League of Nations Man

Hamish Ross

Pen & Sword
MILITARY
AN IMPRINT OF PEN & SWORD BOOKS LTD.
YORKSHIRE – PHILADELPHIA

First published in Great Britain in 2018 by
Pen & Sword Military
An imprint of
Pen & Sword Books Ltd
Yorkshire - Philadelphia

Copyright © Hamish Ross, 2018

ISBN 978 1 52672 805 0

The right of Hamish Ross to be identified as Author of this work has been asserted by him in accordance with the Copyright, Designs and Patents Act 1988.

A CIP catalogue record for this book is
available from the British Library.

All rights reserved. No part of this book may be reproduced or transmitted in any form or by any means, electronic or mechanical including photocopying, recording or by any information storage and retrieval system, without permission from the Publisher in writing.

Printed and bound in England
By TJ International Ltd.

Pen & Sword Books Ltd incorporates the Imprints of Pen & Sword Books Archaeology, Atlas, Aviation, Battleground, Discovery, Family History, History, Maritime, Military, Naval, Politics, Railways, Select, Transport, True Crime, Fiction, Frontline Books, Leo Cooper, Praetorian Press, Seaforth Publishing, Wharncliffe and White Owl.

For a complete list of Pen & Sword titles please contact

PEN & SWORD BOOKS LIMITED
47 Church Street, Barnsley, South Yorkshire, S70 2AS, England
E-mail: enquiries@pen-and-sword.co.uk
Website: www.pen-and-sword.co.uk
or
PEN AND SWORD BOOKS
1950 Lawrence Rd, Havertown, PA 19083, USA
E-mail: Uspen-and-sword@casematepublishers.com
Website: www.penandswordbooks.com

Contents

Acknowledgements		vii
Glossary		ix
Chapter One	Noble Purpose	1
Chapter Two	In the Field	17
Chapter Three	Behind Toothed Wire	35
Chapter Four	Prison Camp Lines	51
Chapter Five	Gatekeeper	71
Chapter Six	Princeton	95
Chapter Seven	Standard-Bearer	115
Chapter Eight	The Long Day's Task is Done	137
Epilogue		143
Afterword		147
Appendix I	The Christ of Mory	151
Appendix II	The Chestnuts	161
Appendix III	A Voice from the Past	163
Bibliography		167
Index		169

Acknowledgements

The source of the Bowman Papers is Glasgow University Archive, and I would very much like to highlight the efficiency and courtesy of the archive staff. Additional material comes from the Seeley G. Mudd Manuscript Library branch of Princeton University Library, from the Mitchell Library Glasgow, from Edinburgh University Archive and from the *Bundesarchiv-Bildarchiv* Koblenz.

I am very grateful for the support of A.A. Bowman's grandchildren, Marjorie Stewart, Janet Macfie, Lydia Bowman and Alastair Gillespie, all of whom shared photographs and documents with me. In addition, Marjorie has written the Afterword.

I also wish to thank A.A. Bowman's niece, Virginia Crawford, for memories of her early years in Princeton and Glasgow.

I would also like to thank Colonel Bobby Steele, TD DL for making available the records in the Royal Highland Fusiliers Museum (the RHF is the successor regiment to the HLI and the Royal Scots Fusiliers).

Finally, my thanks to Joseph Russo, PhD candidate in German, School of Modern Languages & Cultures University of Glasgow, for translating from the German; and to India Fullarton, Photographic Unit University of Glasgow, for photography.

Glossary

Capt	Captain
CND	Campaign for Nuclear Disarmament
Col	Colonel
DL	Deputy Lieutenant
DSO	Distinguished Service Order
EIS	Educational Institute of Scotland
HLI	Highland Light Infantry
Lt	Lieutenant
Maj	Major
OTC	Officer Training Corps
RA	Royal Artillery
RAF	Royal Air Force
RAMC	Royal Army Medical Corps
RE	Royal Engineers
RHF	Royal Highland Fusiliers
RSA	Royal Society of Arts
SCM	Student Christian Movement
TA	Territorial Army
TD	Territorial Decoration
WAAC	Women's Army Auxiliary Corps
WEA	Workers' Educational Association

Chapter One

Noble Purpose

And to be a soldier?
Such is his noble purpose.

William Shakespeare,
All's Well That Ends Well

Billowing grey and dark clouds from the coast rolled in above the breached line at the River Lys in Nord-Pas-de-Calais on that 9th day of April 1918. Scores of allied prisoners were formed up in a column in front of the breastwork trenches. They had not been fed since the day before, were exhausted after ten hours of bombardment and confused by the swiftness of their capture. Some seemed to be asleep on their feet, some still wore their helmets and some had field dressings on their wounds. No one spoke. They were to be led out, marched away from the front to a railway junction beyond artillery range and transported into Germany.

Their guards were support troops, not the storm troops who pierced the defences, and their field grey uniforms were unstained by the battlefield; they could have come from another realm or dropped from the cloud canopy. The *Feldwebel* in charge of them fingered the whistle attached to a lanyard that went round his collar, looked around him, was satisfied with their state of readiness, blew one blast and signalled them forward. The column began to move very slowly; they went along a side track, away from the supply routes for the front. It was as though they were mourners at some vast funeral procession, except that they 'left behind the dying and the dead'.

One of the prisoners was Archie Bowman, a lieutenant in the HLI. 'My vote was cast for a fight to the finish, but Mr Cuthbertson who was in command ordered the surrender. I do not blame him. He is a splendid fellow, and was wounded in two places. But to me the act of surrender was almost unendurable.'

The words of a die-hard warrior? Well, he was a 35-year-old family man, he stood 5ft 8in in height, had a record of frail health, and in the country he left to become a soldier – had the term been current then – he would have been called an egghead. Professor Archibald Allan Bowman held the Stuart Chair of Logic at Princeton, one of America's prestigious Ivy League universities, and he had been given leave of absence to join the British army.

When hostilities broke out in 1914, the United States wanted nothing to do with Europe's wars; according to President Woodrow Wilson it would remain neutral in 'thought and deed'. At Princeton, Bowman kept up with the war news, given the limited extent to which the newspapers reported it, and from February until May 1915 he cut out a series of reports on it from the *New York Times*.

An expat academic in America holding tenure on a salary of $3,500 a year, he might well have stayed put for the duration, but not Bowman. The right thing for him, he believed, was to serve his country in its hour of need. There was no way round it. He felt, he said: 'Like Luther, "I can do no other."' However, he had a wife and child.

Mabel Stewart and Archie Bowman were married on 24 December 1912. Mabel was 25 and Archie was 29. He had just taken up his appointment at Princeton at the beginning of the 1912/13 academic session, and he came back to Glasgow at the Christmas vacation for the wedding. Mabel had been a student of his when he taught at the University of Glasgow before going to Princeton. It was a marriage based on love; they were very close as a couple. When they were apart, in her letters to him, Archie was 'My Most Dearly Loved', sometimes 'Dear Heart', and in his letters to her, Mabel was 'My Own Most Precious Darling' or 'Most Dearly Beloved'. So he knew, in those first few years of marriage, that if he felt strongly about where his duty lay, Mabel would support him, although she would be left carrying the heavy end: on her own looking after a baby, continually worrying about him and frightened at the prospect of becoming a young widow. Yet she did it uncomplainingly. As Archie put it: 'My personal eagerness is splendidly sustained by the backing I get all the time from my wife – no small war service.'

So he applied to Princeton University for leave of absence to join the British army. Princeton granted Professor Bowman's request. He would be given leave of absence for the academic year 1915–16 at half salary; his work would be partly shared among the department and partly covered by hiring a half-time assistant at $500. The arrangement would be reviewed in a year's time.

He continued teaching and carrying out his administrative duties until the end of session. He made arrangements for the sub-lease of the house they were renting and he booked a cabin on the SS *Tuscania*, a new luxury passenger liner of the Anchor Line, sailing from New York on 24 July to Glasgow. They packed their belongings in two trunks, travelled to New York and stayed at the Hotel Chelsea on West 23rd Street in readiness for their departure.

They were both anxious about making the Atlantic crossing because just two months earlier, in May, a German U-boat had torpedoed the Cunard liner *Lusitania*, and more than 1,000 civilians had perished. This act of war was given much attention in the American newspapers.

On the morning of Saturday, 24 July 1915, there was a sense of excitement in the air on the decks of the *Tuscania*; excitement yet a feeling of apprehension as passengers gathered at the ship's rails. The order was given, and the stem and stern ropes were released from the harbour bollards. Moving slowly at first through the busy harbour, the elegant liner got under way. Many passengers stayed on deck to gaze on the city skyline of Manhattan that had been changing so much in the past fifteen years. Gradually Manhattan and then the Statue of Liberty diminished in size as the *Tuscania* gathered speed out into the open ocean.

As the voyage progressed, Bowman felt that the tension they had been under was easing. He put this down to the attitude and actions of the ship's crew, who were nonchalant and remained nonchalant throughout the voyage. Captain Peter Maclean made a point of being seen on deck: he posed for groups of passengers and had his photo taken with them, and he held baby Ian Bowman for the camera. With the crew's relaxed attitude, Bowman noted that they gave less and less thought to 'the submarine terror', and he felt this seemed to be the case generally among the rest of the passengers.

The new ship was destined to become widely-known in the course of the war. In September she went to the rescue of passengers on a burning Greek steamer, and two years later, by then requisitioned by the British government as a troopship, the *Tuscania* was in the news again when she evaded a U-boat and a German surface raider.

As it turned out, however, the professionalism of the crew was really working in harmony with a fickle shipmate – Fortune – and at Hoboken, New Jersey on 29 January 1918, with the last of 2,000 American troops embarked, it jumped ship but left a token behind.

The timing of that crossing held an ill omen and on 5 February, almost three years to the day from her maiden voyage, in the dark waters between Islay and Rathlin Island, the ship was stalked by a U-boat. The attack came suddenly; they picked up no warning signs. At 18.40, *UB-77*'s commander *Kapitänleutnant* Wilhelm Meyer fired two torpedoes: the first missed, but the second hit the ship by the engine room on the starboard side. Within minutes she was listing to starboard, but she stayed afloat for hours, long enough for British warships to rescue 90 per cent of the total ship's complement. Finally, bow-first, she slid under the waves; there was an explosion muffled by the waters, and the *Tuscania* plunged to the bottom with the loss of 230 lives.

However, that lay hidden in the future when, on Monday, 2 August 1915, under a pale blue sky with banks of cumulus drifting in from the west, at the end of her transatlantic crossing the *Tuscania* steamed 'through the gorgeous portals of the Clyde' and up her home river, lined with shipyards. As the river narrowed, the air resounded with volleys of hammering from the riveters, and as the ship came abreast of Stephens of Linthouse, the captain ordered one blast on the horn, a salute to the yard and the men that built her. Then she was berthed at Yorkhill Quay.

Tired after the long voyage, Archie and Mabel with their baby headed for 77 Montgomerie Street, Glasgow, which was her parental home.

Archie had been born in Crummock Cottage in Beith, Ayrshire with no silver spoon in his mouth: he was the eldest of a family of five, his father was an Evangelical Union clergyman, and the family income was never more than £100 per year. Archie had been an excellent scholar at Beith Academy and Spiers School. However, when he was in his last year at school his father died, meaning that Archie had to help his mother run the house, and he had to help his brothers and sister with their schooling. It looked as if his prospects of going up to university were doomed, but the headmaster of Spiers School took the initiative and raised a fund from among local people and well-wishers and with this and a bursary he won in the entrance examination, Archie entered the University of Glasgow. His mother moved the family into Glasgow, having to take in lodgers to make ends meet, and Archie tutored students to bring extra money in to the home.

He had had a taste of army life already: after graduating with Second-Class Honours in Classics and First-Class Honours in Philosophy, he was taken on as assistant and lecturer in the Department of Logic and Metaphysics. In the long vacations during the next few years he studied in Germany at the universities of Berlin, Heidelberg and Leipzig, and during those years he became very aware of a militaristic culture in the air as the country was feeling its new industrial strength; he read some of the thoughts of Heinrich von Treitschke – a historian, political writer and a member of the Reichstag in his day, who had believed in colonialism and was hostile to the British Empire – and Bowman formed the view that, in time, there would be war and he should be ready to serve. So in 1908 he joined the university's OTC and in July 1910, according to the wording of the Court at St James's, 'Our Trusty and Well-beloved Archibald Allan Bowman' received the King's Commission in the Territorial Forces, but of course he resigned his commission when he went to the United States.

Rested and restored after the Atlantic crossing, Bowman reported for service at Maryhill Barracks, the depot of the Highland Light Infantry, the City of Glasgow regiment. A medical was arranged for him, but he was passed fit for military service without undergoing it, although they gave him an eyesight test. The medical officer, who had known him from their days at Territorial camps, said that he was aware of Archie Bowman's level of fitness. After that cursory preliminary, Bowman was graded B1 and told to await his appointment as a second lieutenant on the Unattached List.

Two of his brothers were already in uniform and on active service in France: Arthur was in the Royal Engineers and Jim in the Royal Artillery. Mabel had three brothers in uniform: Ronald in the RAMC, Jim in the infantry and Norman was training with the Canadian forces.

Yet three weeks later Bowman found himself still waiting his appointment on the Unattached List, and at that time, both from reading the newspapers and from personal experience, he felt there was a failure at government level to tackle what had to be done in a time of national emergency. It showed itself in a lackadaisical attitude on the part of officialdom. The problem, he felt, percolated down from the very top, from the War Cabinet. It seemed to him that Prime Minister Lloyd George was 'effective only as a member of a cabinet and not as the transcendent leader of a people.'

On 22 August he wrote to his colleague and friend at Princeton, a fellow Scot, Norman Kemp Smith, who came from Dundee and was the McCosh Professor of Philosophy. Bowman and Kemp Smith were part of a long tradition of Scots teaching philosophy at Princeton, a tradition that went back as far as the eighteenth century. Kemp Smith had been in post since 1906; he had been interviewed for the job in a hotel on Princes Street, Edinburgh by the president of Princeton, Woodrow Wilson, the man who was by then president of the United States of America.

Kemp Smith, like Bowman, wanted to serve his country. He was eleven years older than Bowman and felt he was probably too old for military service. However, there were bound to be opportunities in government departments for a man who was a fluent German scholar and knew the country. Bowman promised that he would try to find out about suitable work for him, but after making enquiries he was not optimistic: 'It seems to me that at the present moment you would have great difficulty in procuring anything that would be worthwhile.'

Bowman gave him his assessment of the state of affairs:

> The half-hearted methods hitherto employed are little short of an insult to the intelligence of the people. Recruiting by advertisement and temperance lecture by exalted personages border too closely on the nature of jokes... There is something very pathetic and very humorous in the complex relations at present existing between the nation and the executive. First of all there is the fundamental substratum of loyalty. The country as a whole is pledged (spiritually pledged) to support the government to the uttermost. 'Yes,' say the ministers, 'we know it. We know your splendid loyalty, and therefore we are going to trust you to do everything voluntarily. We will treat you to a display of beautifully designed and coloured posters, conceived in the most sentimental vein

and specially designed to appeal to the great heart of the democracy. We will present to you the infinitely moving spectacle of King George and Kitchener foreswearing their whisky – "if necessary" – in the full assurance that you will be unable to resist such a beautiful example.'

Bowman was not exaggerating about public policy being treated as a bit of a joke. There was evidence of it in the city to which he had just returned. A Glasgow evening newspaper, the *Evening Times*, ran a series of humorous stories by the novelist Neil Munro centred on a character he called Erchie, a Glasgow worthy, commenting, often to a friend, on local and national weighty events. One of the stories appearing in the newspaper was spun round the news of the king's foreswearing whisky, only, in the telling, it becomes magnified through folklore to include an act of parliament closing all pubs:

> The King himsel's teetotal noo; no' a drop o' onything in the hoose for him but buttermilk, or maybe a bottle or two o' raspberry cordial. 'What'll ye hae, your Majesty?' says his butler, bringing in the tray at nicht. 'I suppose there's naething for't but buttermilk as usual,' says the King.' 'Richt-o!' says the butler, and slaps him doon a jugful. It's a lesson to us a', Duffy.

As for the idea of closing all pubs, the local sage finds something deviously clever in this policy. 'When it's generally understood that the only place in Europe where ye can get a tot o' rum is in the trenches, every high-spirited young man'll 'list.'

From his own experience, Bowman found unnecessary delays in processing his commission. The OTC headquarters in Glasgow was now devoted to the training and supply of officers. He went along only to find it closed: the staff were on holiday! He contacted the commanding officer at his home and he pursued the matter for him, but then there was a further delay of a fortnight. Bowman followed this up, and he learned that Captain Clive, the head of the War Office department processing the granting of commissions, was on holiday. Clive, as it happened, was someone Bowman remembered well, a man who had been at Territorial camps with him and 'it was notorious then that he was a man innocent of the very meaning of work!' Basically, Bowman reckoned the government was too slow for the spirit abroad in the country, and he felt there was really only one way in which it could take the necessary steps in a great emergency: 'It must <u>act</u>.'

His application for a commission began with delay and frustration and continued in a style that comes with bureaucratic inefficiency. That first September, in his last days as a civilian, he wrote again to Kemp Smith at Princeton:

Well, the vacation is drawing to a close, and your thoughts will be turning Princeton-wards again. If I had a peaceful spirit I would envy you; but there is in me a pent-up store of restlessness that nothing but action can assuage. My commission has been granted, but in a form far from gratifying. My training and qualifications have gone for nothing and I have to start all over again on the lowest rung of the ladder under a man who was once one of my students (an indifferent one) and who four years ago got his own military training as a cadet in my company. I don't mind the juniority, but I fear that my own further military training will be in poor hands. The camp to which I am to be sent (Stobbs) has also a very bad reputation. It consists of officers exclusively and is said to be in a badly demoralised condition – discipline being very slack. What I wanted was to be posted to a unit, where I could generally work up a genuine control over my men – a control based on mutual knowledge and respect.

Past training having counted for nothing, Bowman was commissioned as a second lieutenant in the 13th HLI. Before he joined his regiment there was first a six-week course of training in fieldwork and musketry in the Glasgow area. The group he was in were mainly ex-OTC comrades and they got on well, and the course was well-run. Bowman worked hard throughout: 'I don't think anyone in the class worked as hard as I did' and it got him good results in the eight written and practical tests that were set. He found that he was working longer hours than at Princeton but he was surprised 'how much lighter this kind of work is than philosophy.' The hardest part of the course for him was the physical demands of rapid musketry work: 'I had to practise with the rifle for hours and hours at home in the evenings.' However, he got through the course with flying colours.

The contrast when he went to Stobbs could not have been more marked: the training was useless, he felt, and discipline was non-existent. Fortunately for him he did not have to endure the whole course for his battalion took him on its strength right away and he joined it at Catterick in Yorkshire.

It was a huge camp with about 2,000 huts and there he found he was in with a mixed lot; some of the eleven men he shared a hut with had VD. One night it seemed to him that the whole battalion had a bacchanalian warm-up for war:

> I hardly expected at a time like this to see British officers wallowing in the mud outside the mess, or to see the senior officer present reduced to a condition of helplessness and the whole batch of a hundred or more officers of the regiment in a state of extreme intoxication.

There were some exceptions, though. Bowman was strictly teetotal; if others took 'an occasional refreshment' that was their choice, but he was abstemious. Yet although he found it a sorry sight, it did not get Bowman down – he seemed to be on a high of his own – 'I have such a superabounding store of physical and mental energy that I find it impossible to escape high spirits even in the most distressing circumstances.'

The 13th Battalion HLI had been turned into a training battalion, training men to replace losses in France in two other battalions. Bowman put in a request to move into civilian accommodation so that he could bring Mabel. The colonel supported him and permission was granted. He wired Mabel with the news and soon the family of three was in a small house in Richmond. Bowman walked the couple of miles or so each way to the camp. It was the only physical exercise he got in his new role, which was the tactical instruction of men in the last stage of training, and much of it was in the form of diagrammatic presentation which was right up Bowman's street.

When he was a young schoolboy he had become seriously ill. There were fears for his life; his younger brother Alex, who in adulthood became a doctor, reckoned it began as acute rheumatism and this was followed by acute nephritis – inflammation of the kidneys – from which many children died in those days. After the illness, Archie required a period of convalescence: a house with four younger siblings was not the place for it and he was sent to Perth, to his maternal grandfather's family. Archie subsequently returned to Perth during school holidays and he spent a lot of time in the art gallery and by a bridge over the River Tay, sketching. His uncle, Alexander King, who was in practice as a solicitor in Perth, had an interest in art, and through him Archie had some tutoring by the artist William Proudfoot.

Bowman enjoyed the work at Catterick; it was an eye-opener for him, the responsiveness of a very different constituency of learners from what he was used to in his civilian job. 'I find soldiers a splendid audience, and enjoy lecturing them immensely. Altogether my relations with the rank and file are extraordinarily happy, and when at the end of a lecture I put questions, the men respond with eagerness and intelligence that would surprise you.'

However, there was another cadre in the camp of which he had a low opinion: the middle-ranking officers drafted back into service by the War Office. He described them as 'the curse of the army.' His superior officer was one of them: a Major Anderson who was middle-aged and had years of service behind him; he had several decorations, including the Boer war ribbon. He had others as well but, as he told Bowman,

> he had removed them at the beginning of the war, for fear they should attract attention and get him sent to the front. His one object in life is to

avoid work and get fox-hunting. For a man who has been through the Boer war and the Boxer expedition, he is grotesquely ignorant of everything military, and has welcomed me with open arms because I can relieve him of the impossible task of lecturing.

One day the colonel informed them that a General Farquharson was coming to visit the battalion, and they were told that every company should be engaged in some activity during the time of the visit: one, drill and musketry; another, trench-digging, and so on. Bowman's major suggested that their company be absent on a route march, but the colonel ruled that out; the major then proposed that they be lectured, but that was vetoed. Holding off until the battalion was about to parade for the general, the major prevailed on the colonel and

> suddenly, without a moment's warning, I was ordered to march the company off and lecture them. When I asked for a subject, I was told anything would do, but I was to draw some 'damned diagram' which would make an impression on the general. The army has taught me to be a desperado, but I had a few minutes' nervous excitement. The question uppermost in my mind was whether I should lecture on an old subject, where I was thoroughly at home, or should improvise an entirely new lecture which would follow naturally in the series I was giving. I decided on the latter course, altho' I had not even begun to prepare for this lecture. I think my somewhat highly-keyed condition was partly responsible for the result; but once I got started, I found I had every detail at my finger-ends – including figures – and the natural logic of the subject carried me from sequence to sequence in a way that surprised even myself. When the staff-captain arrived to announce the approach of the general – there were really two of them – I had full steam up and nothing could have stopped me. Suddenly the major's voice rang out 'Attention' and I had to pause momentarily while a misty cavalcade of senior officers filed in in a dreadful silence. I had a dim image of a grey figure in a gold-braided cap, and a voice instructing me to 'Carry on'. I carried on and paid no attention to the august audience, and all I know is that when I finished I was surrounded by a group of silent and attentive Tommies, but generals, colonel, majors, staff and other captains, and even subalterns had vanished on their rounds. I had the satisfaction of hearing that the general was well impressed with the performance.

However, Bowman's bravura performance before General Farquharson turned out to work against his own inclinations: he wanted to be posted on active service;

however, impressing the general resulted in a 'That chap should be posted to an established training unit. Damned good diagram' kind of profundity. So Bowman was soon after posted to the 2nd HLI and attached to the 52nd Training Battalion based at Windygates in Fife, on the north shore of the Firth of Forth.

There, he was responsible for training officers. He ran courses in tactics: night operations, methods of deployment, reconnoitring patrols and sentry systems, among others. One of the benefits of the posting was that he was again allowed to live in civilian accommodation and he brought Mabel and Ian. They rented a house in the town of Leven. That meant that they were able to invite guests round. One evening Mabel invited her best friend Jennie Aitken, and she also invited a friend of Archie's, Harry Mackay, a fellow HLI officer, for a little get-together and to share their meagre fare.

Overdue though it was, in July 1916 he was promoted to lieutenant and given command of a company. The company was about 200 strong: 'I've four subalterns under me, three sergeant-majors, and about forty non-commissioned officers.' He was out in the field from morning till night superintending the work of subordinates, and he began to learn the art of leaving the details to others.

Later in the year Bowman was told that he could be nominated for a staff appointment at the front, but he turned it down 'as the appointment was in the intelligence department, which to my mind connoted spies and other things alien to my taste and capacity.' What he wanted was a field posting.

It was a strange existence, living as a family: Mabel was pregnant again, the new arrival was expected in December; Archie anticipating the wonder of a new life in the home, and in his working day preparing men to kill.

In 1916, the British had evolved a tactic of carrying out raids on specific targets. It was said to be 'a leading method in the wearing-down process' and it involved close-quarter fighting with the bayonet, but the men were being trained in one aspect that Bowman found unsettling: killing an already wounded enemy. He gave a detailed description of the tactic in a letter to Norman Kemp Smith.

The two had kept in regular contact, and since Bowman's arrival in this country in 1915 only to find what he thought was a national administration in idling mode, the government had moved through the gears: it introduced conscription for the first time in the country's history, and became more sophisticated in judging the skills and abilities they needed to supplement those of the civil service in various government departments. There was now no problem about a suitable role for an academic like Kemp Smith. So he too took the same road as Bowman and applied to the university for leave of absence to serve his country at war and he too was granted it. He came to the UK and was assigned to work in the Ministry of Information. His wife and daughter would follow and join him later.

Bowman described the aforementioned tactic with an exemplar diagram of a target, a sap, which was a long trench originating behind the enemy line and extending under cover of night to the British line. The target had been spotted by aerial reconnaissance. About 120 men and 3 officers would be selected for the raid, withdrawn from the front and given special training, and so a new element was introduced into the training courses. Bowman told Kemp Smith of his part in the development:

> The war has reached an almost incredibly savage stage. I have been doing more bayonet-fighting of late, and have been struck with this. Our men are deliberately taught never to spare a fallen enemy but to kill every time and by every and any method. A special chapter in advanced bayonet-fighting is devoted to what are frankly called 'dirty tricks'. We have a magnificent head instructor. He is not only an expert bayonet-man, but is the gentlest and most courteous of soldiers. It is a strange paradox to see this really gentle and chivalrous soul expound and emphasise the 'dirty tricks' of bayonet-fighting.

Mabel's baby was a girl; she was born on 2 December 1916 and they named her Mary Isabel, but she was known as Maisie.

Then early in 1917, there were changes to Bowman's duties which meant leaving the camp for some time and Mabel took the children back to her parents' home in Glasgow. Bowman was appointed grenade officer, and later attended a course on anti-gas tactics. Also he was sent to France, to a base camp for a stint as a draft-conducting officer. It was not yet active service, but it was a change from Leven where, as a result of policy changes at higher level, he was unhappy. He told Kemp Smith why:

> Since I saw you in mid-summer my work has been depressing almost beyond endurance, and my anxieties have been many and great. The whole system has been in the melting pot for months, and the changes of policy on the part of the authorities are absolutely kaleidoscopic. My company for months has been simply a clearing-house for passing bodies of men, and my work has been little else than receiving mobs of heterogeneous individuals, and dealing them out singly and in parcels to destinations all over the kingdom.

He was the only subaltern in command of a company but, finally, he had to relinquish it to a captain. In a letter to Kemp Smith he said: 'Promotion is evidently impossible here. I was told some months ago that my name had been submitted;

but if this is so, nothing has come of it; and my removal from the command of a company removes the only ground on which it could be put up again.' However, he did not lament his lot. He was put in charge of training cadets; they were drawn from all sorts of units, they were of fine calibre, and his work became rewarding again.

Being out in the open air every day could lift his spirits and bring back an affinity with the boyhood wonder of exploring the countryside:

> You know this soldier life, when I am not too pressed with work, revives within me a great sense of romantic joy in nature, with love the dominant magic note in it. I can't explain it but I have had it since I was a boy and it is one of the deepest and purest joys earth can give.

After a leave in Glasgow, he wrote to 'My Sweetheart':

> Ever since I left you so hurriedly at Queen Street Station I've been so full of yearning towards you – just hungering for you as in the old days when each night I had to leave you and I could hardly wait until the morrow brought us together again. Darling, it feels so like those old days, being without you at night. The holiday together, even tho' we seemed to get so little of it together, is simply so beyond expression, dear and precious to the memory – every moment weighted with an infinity of joy, and the joy composed, directly or indirectly, of no other than our love. Glasgow is marvellously dear to me because it is the scene of our first passion, and all over it is haunted with memories sweet and kind; for even what was bitter in those old times is sweet now in the memory, our love having prospered and grown so amazingly out of sweet and bitter roots alike.

In another letter: 'My Mabel, it was an infinitely love-sick man that went off to Leven tonight. Do you remember the old Lesmahagow days…?' He recalled their courting days in Glasgow when, as a young teacher at the university, he saw Mabel off on the tram that would take her to where she worked, and he stood watching the red tail-light of her tramcar disappearing into the night.

With the reality of total war, the ever-present sense of impending loss heightened feelings for home and loved ones, and Bowman reckoned that sooner or later he would be sent to the front. The war seemed far from reaching its conclusion but still kept churning on with the carnage; it could go on for years, and he might end among the lost generation. So when he wrote a letter to Ian so that Ian would get it on his second birthday, Bowman wrote it on two levels. He wrote it in terms of the child's understanding, using the child's vocabulary, but he wrote part of it for the future – for Mabel would keep it – when his son would be at an age of discretion.

Windygates, Wednesday
Evening, May 9th 1917

My Own Dear Ian

Your daddy-man is writing this to you out of a very full heart. He intends you to get it on your second birthday. In another two days you will be two years old; and the two years of your life are two of the most awful years that have ever been since the world began. For in these years more men have been busy killing and trying to kill each other than ever before, and there has been terrible hatred and terrible sorrow in the world. But of all this you know nothing, and it is very well that you do not know it; and I hope you never know it too nearly. For God has given you a merry little heart and glad ways, and you have brought joy immeasurable into very many hearts, and into two hearts in particular, your mother's and your father's. And your gladness and mirthfulness are very, very precious to them and very, very good.

Now I hope that you and Girlie-gee are going to have a splendid day and to romp and play and shout with glee. A birthday is just the time when you should be very happy; because in it you celebrate the day when you were born; and when a boy is born he comes straight from God's hands and is as God made him and so long as he remains that is a great gain to the world. I don't know what special fun Mamminay has in store for you; but I know there'll be some special fun going; and if daddy were there he'd be in the thick of it, romping and dancing about with you, and we'd have a tremendous time. I wonder if there'll be a birthday cake with two candles. If so, you'll have to bring a bit to daddy; and you'll have to tell daddy all about it, and who were at your birthday party and how you danced and romped about and had grand fun.

And now daddy wants to say some special things to you, in case at some later time, when he should want to say them, it might not be possible. And these are the things he wants to say:

I In all things, whether thinking, or deciding or acting, reckon with God. Take Him into account before all else.

II In order to understand God and how He should be taken into account, study Him constantly in the teaching and the life of Jesus.

III If you do that, you will learn these great things: Never be <u>contented</u> with anything short of the very <u>Highest</u> and <u>Best</u>. If you do not attain to it, still, never <u>aim</u> at anything less. Your conscience will tell you if you do.

Although Bowman wrote in terms of Jesus as the lodestar guiding the way to God, he and Mabel did not have Ian and Maisie christened. Bowman did not adhere to religious doctrine.

A few months after Ian's second birthday, on a family holiday, Bowman felt the pangs of time passing and of irretrievable loss. In October, he had been given a week's leave and the family spent it at Tighnabruaich on the Kyles of Bute. It was a rough crossing by steamer on their way home:

> I don't know why it is that some days (not always the most likely) should have such power to move the heart and soul. That day is one of them; the memory of the dark and stormy passage home with the little boy on our knee is overpowering. How I am grudging the passage of time that will gradually take him away from us! Soon it will be no longer necessary to carry him – then no longer possible; lastly he'll slide away into the world where we cannot follow him – the world which itself will be slipping away from us – the new world of the coming generation where we will be half-aliens. What tragedy there is in love, Dear. It's the thing on which life feeds and lives, but all its linked sweetness is at every moment passing thro' our hands and into the mines of an irrecoverable past. Already, since I have known you, an appreciable span of life is gone, and my very soul is turning back with yearning inexpressible to memories that are as precious as life itself. Do you remember, very early, remarking how I always seemed to be looking forward? It is no longer so. Now I am looking back and forward, looking wherever love is to be seen – the love that has beautified our life behind as well as the love that beckons us...

When he returned from that leave, it was to find that policy changes were in place that would separate him from his family: the training battalion was broken up, and Bowman reverted to the 13th HLI, the reserve battalion from which officer reinforcements were drawn for the front line.

He was posted to the 10/11th HLI. He was given embarkation leave and Saturday, 19 January 1918 was his last evening at home with the family. 'Did you know that when we were sitting at that last meal there were moments when I could not have spoken? And when I put our little Maisie to bed it was almost too much for me.'

Later that night, Mabel went with him to Glasgow's St Enoch Station. The platform seemed too small for the crowds: in the soft glow of the gas lamps, khaki and naval greatcoats mingled with the drab civilian wartime dress. The first-class compartment of the overnight train to London was empty, and Mabel sat with him until it was time for it to leave. Then came the moment of parting, 'when that last dear lingering kiss was taken, Beloved, I just sat back and let my mind work, following you on your way home from point to point and realising it all with such vividness.' He had the compartment to himself. 'I was so thankful to be alone. The carriage still bore the sweetness that your being there with me imparted to it.' He then stayed with that sense of her presence until the beat of the train wheels sent him to sleep.

Chapter Two

In the Field

*A cheerless landscape gray, and the profound
Loneliness of the battlefield.*
A.A. Bowman,
Sonnets from a Prison Camp

Forty-eight hours after Archie said goodbye to Mabel, he was in France. It was a mild January night with a bright moon. He was taken to a reception camp not far from the harbour. It was the same camp that he had been to when he served as a draft-conducting officer, only now it had a mess and, compared with rationing back home, in the reception camp in war-torn France they seemed to be living off the fat of the land. He told Norman Kemp Smith about it.

Since his assignment to the Ministry of Information, Kemp Smith told Bowman that he had been 'commandeered' into organizing propaganda aimed at the American public: 'Macneile Dixon is in charge of it. Please, however, do not mention nature of my work.' The Macneile Dixon in charge of the section was William Macneile Dixon, Professor of English Language and Literature at Glasgow University, and well-known as joint editor of *The English Parnassus: An Anthology Chiefly of Longer Poems* which was often a prescribed textbook at universities. One outcome of the Macneile Dixon/Kemp Smith collaboration was to be a thirty-two-page pamphlet entitled 'Know your ally: a brief record of Great Britain's contributions to the cause of democracy and liberty.'

Kemp Smith was meantime staying at Heath Mansions in Hampstead, and he invited Bowman to stay overnight on his way to Folkestone en route for France. Bowman arrived in the early afternoon. Kemp Smith gave him a warm welcome, and they had a long talk. Due to food rationing, they partook of a frugal evening meal: 'bread and cheese or jam and apple charlotte.' Then they took a walk to Highgate after the meal, came back and had a rest.

Bowman then did an hour's work on the proof of a book that Kemp Smith had written. It was a philosophical work on the German philosopher Immanuel Kant, entitled *A Commentary to Kant's Critique of Pure Reason*. Kemp Smith had completed his research for it and had written it when he was at Princeton, but it was being published in the UK. Of course, in these times, one had to be sensitive about anything with a German connotation; there were many expressions of anti-German feeling in Britain during the war (much more so than in the Second World War). There were instances of shop fronts with German names being damaged, signs defaced, and only six months earlier King George V had changed the family name from Saxe-Coburg-Gotha to Windsor – *The Times* carried a royal proclamation to that effect – so as he was going over the page proofs, Kemp Smith gave final thought to how he would forestall possible sniping from newspaper columnists for being unpatriotic in publishing a book about a German philosopher during the hostilities. In his Preface, he conceded that some might think an apology was due for its appearance during the hostilities, then deftly turned it around with an anecdote from another war – that had a sub-text about the flexibility of mind of British generals – by alluding to one of Britain's former enemies, General Smuts, who 'has himself told us that on his raid into Cape Colony in the South African War he carried with him for evening reading *The Critique of Pure Reason*. Is it surprising that our British generals, pitted against so unconventional an opponent, should have been worsted in the battle of wits?' Also in his Preface, signed January 1918, Kemp Smith included his colleague Professor Archibald Allan Bowman in his thanks.

The next night Bowman was in France on active service. The first meal he had at the reception camp was in startling contrast to the bread-and-cheese offering at Kemp Smith's: he was given a six-course dinner, 'each course was exquisitely served by attractive WAACs.'

It was a few days before he left the base to join his unit, and one evening he went to a cinema to see a French documentary film about the war. The picture-house was packed, chiefly with Belgian and British soldiers. 'The interesting point was that the moral tone of it all was so far above what you would see in a British cinema. There was a complete absence of those grotesque pictures, and the bulk of the show consisted of topical pictures interspersed with letter-press of appropriate nature.' The film was about the training of French soldiers, the organization of French industry and patriotic shots of French heroes being decorated. However, there was also acknowledgement of the allied forces: the British, Belgian, Italian and American, all accompanied by snatches of their national music. 'I was interested in the grave moral purpose of the show. Then we walked out to camp under exquisite moonlight – a full moon sailing in a rippling sea of fleecy clouds.'

Bowman joined his unit on 29 January. The 10/11th HLI had been stationed south of Arras since the beginning of the month. It was dark and it was raining. They were put up in tents and there was no orderly to carry his equipment; he had to do it himself and that jolt to what he thought was his due left him with 'a new sympathy for men who make their bread by bearing other men's burdens.'

He wrote to Kemp Smith: 'I have been posted to one of the 2 battalions I sincerely wished to avoid.' In another letter to him he said: 'I promised to mention the name of my CO. Well, his name is Lt Col R F Forbes. I have never, I think, known a case of a man so unanimously execrated by his officers as he is.' For his part, though, he found both a friendly welcome and the CO supportive, but there was no induction period under the eye of an experienced officer:

> My first tour of duty in the trenches was most interesting. The details I will reserve for some future occasion. Suffice it to say that I was sent on duty straight away on arrival, that I had my first experience of coming under fire in No Man's Land the same night on patrol work, that I commanded a strong point under intense artillery fire shortly after and that on evacuating the trenches we had to pass thro' an enemy barrage. The psychical effect of shell fire on my mind I found to be a pleasurable exhilaration and a strong stirring of the primitive instinct to fight. The greatest hardship of the trenches I found to be the want of sleep. I had only a few hours of the latter in five days, and the conditions under which this was snatched (sleeping with all one's clothes, and above all with heavy trench boots on), made it somewhat of an unrestful order. The deep dugouts (our sleeping quarters were in the Hindenburg tunnel, 30 to 50 feet underground) also had somewhat of a horror for me, as had the continual working parties in the mud. We were always getting embogged, and one night it took nearly an hour's desperate labour to dig one of my men out of the gluey composition. The following night I went in myself, tho' a couple of stalwart fellows managed to extricate me.

The Hindenburg tunnel had been part of the Siegfried Line and had been captured from the Germans. On that first tour of duty Bowman desperately wanted some sleep; he could not leave his post, so he went down into the depths of the men's dugout to try to get some sleep there. In a letter to Mabel's brother Johnnie, he described the scene deep in the bowels of the Siegfried Line:

> One thing that gives me the horrors, and that was the men's dugout. It was situated in a tunnel 40 or 50 feet below the surface of the ground, and so big and steep were the steps leading down that one had to go down backwards clinging to a rope. The steps and the floor consisted of chalk clay, and when the men were in, the odour of human bodies, blending with the close damp smell of the soil and the oniony aroma left by the dinners, rendered the place quite nauseating.

Although the line at Arras was quiet, the artillery was not silent. Every night the sky was lit up by the flashes of gunfire, and in a heavy strafe the guns roared in a continuous peal for ten minutes or so and, when the weather allowed, there was also continuous air reconnaissance.

A recurring note that comes through in the early months in France is his confidence that he had disproved the merchants of gloom who predicted that he would never stand up to the rigours of trench warfare. In one letter he leads in to it by describing the way men can get used to constant bombardment and shut it out:

> The attitude of the men under violent shelling was most interesting. They were ordered to crouch down under the parapet, and there they were, smoking cigarettes with a look of sheer boredom on their faces, waiting for it to blow over. – Active service conditions seem to agree with me splendidly, and the prophecies of the doctor at Windygates that if I came over in the winter I would simply crumple up on arrival seem ludicrous. As a matter of fact I seem in far better form than any number of the men. During the cold snap quite a lot of the officers were quite done up, and had to take to bed for a few days.

He quickly got used to the conditions of trench warfare and did not bemoan his lot; he simply accepted the conditions of life as he found them and went with them: 'The day was wet and miserable, but I determined to make the most of it; I brushed, washed and shaved in half a mug of water; and spent the rest of the day in observation.'

One afternoon, a self-assured Lieutenant Bowman took a walk across country in an area that had been fought over months earlier. In their tactical withdrawal from the Hindenburg Line, the enemy had laid the land bare. It was now a treeless waste of devastation and the infrastructure had been destroyed: roads and bridges had been blown up to impede an army's advance; telegraph wires strewed the earth. There were the deserted trenches that many men had died defending and attacking, and the fields that had once produced rich yields were now vast tracts of mud, pitted with shell-holes.

Towards dusk he was returning to the dugout when he came across a gigantic heap of rubble that had once been the village church. Standing out against the darkening sky, in a macabre juxtaposition of symbols, was the god of war mocking a broken Christ: on top of the rubble was a flagstaff with the flapping pennant of some division or corps and just below it 'a huge and very artistic crucifix, the figure of Christ, shockingly realistic, hanging by one hand to the cross and swaying gently in the breeze.' To Bowman, 'It seemed as if a new iniquity had been added to crucifixion; and yet in it all the prevailing feeling in my mind was that of Christ triumphant.' The scene made such an impact on him that he later wrote about it in narrative verse (see Appendix I).

For the rest of the winter months, patrol activity, constructing a series of new trenches and platoon training were the mainstay of the battalion's preparations for what was expected to be the enemy's spring offensive.

Some preparations had to be made at night and towards the end of February, late one evening Bowman went by train through what seemed a spectral landscape, with a ghostly moon above, to what had been a settlement where the earth had given up its dead:

> Last night was one of the most tiring experiences I have had since coming to France. We marched to the entraining point – about 600 of us – and there entrained in 3 trains. The journey up in the gray twilight thro' the wilderness was weird beyond description – miles and miles of desolate country overgrown with gray grass, with here and there the jaws of mysterious underground works, abandoned German trenches and magnificent systems of wire, camouflaged positions etc. The railway was operated by Americans and had something of the slap-dash American character about it. I rode in the last truck of the first train. The gradient proved almost too much for our tractor, and when we slowed down, the second train quite regularly came bumping into us, and I had to shout forward to the men to hold on till the bump was over. It was almost dark when we disentrained and were led by guides of the REs to our tasks. The men worked very well. The soil was pure white chalk and showed very plainly in the diffused moonlight. It was just such a night as I anticipated – clouds scurrying under the wind across the face of a two-thirds full moon. Every now and again a Very light went up along the front line or a gun boomed out; but the night was very quiet. Close by was a graveyard with the dead partly disinterred. It was somewhat wearisome walking up and down examining the work and I grew tired and footsore. My men did so well, however, that about 10 o'clock the RE officer passed our section as finished, and we tailed off, dumped picks and shovels, and proceeded to the entraining point, where the other companies gradually assembled. Then a long wait ensued. No sign of the train… It turned out that the train had run on to the terminus and the engine had run over the end of the line and was now fast in the soft soil. We found the American engineer working furiously at it, and I was sent up with 60 men to give a hand. But after a long effort the Engineer sergeant reported to our major that it would take another 3 or 4 hours to get the engine on. So we had to turn back, fall the men in and start off on the long tramp back to camp. It was most pleasant to me to hear the good old American accent again, and I could not enter into the general objurgations that were levelled at the

heads of all Americans. The march back was done in splendid style tho' the men must have been dead-dog tired. It was most weird, passing dug-outs and graves and ruined houses all showing ghostly in the moonlight. We got in after a swinging march about 2 o'clock; and by the time I had seen the men supplied with tea and some supper myself it was 3am. I must say a rare supper was awaiting us – omelette with chopped ham in the middle. This morning I wakened with a slight headache, which is now better. However, there is nothing to get up for and we all slept in and had the luxury of breakfast in bed. As it is now afternoon we'll soon have to be getting ready for tonight. We go up again, as also tomorrow night on similar work. I believe I could get off one or other of these nights, but am anxious to go for the sake of the experience. I want to read up the subject a little before starting. There is a remarkable lack of organisation and proper arrangements in all these matters, and I feel that if I ever get the chance I could arrange things much better than at present.

The next night the working parties were out again. Bowman came back in the last truck with the American NCO in charge of the train, 'and we had a long talk about America. He is a conductor on the Hartford railway, lives in Boston and runs between there and Hartford.' The American sergeant told him that the engineers' headquarters of the American corps was at a village not very far off, and that he would find Princeton and Harvard men there. 'So I'm thinking of walking over some day soon and making enquiries.'

On 1 March, the 10/11th HLI moved to Berles-au-Bois, about 15 kilometres south-west of Arras. It was an attractive wooded area that had not been laid waste. It was a welcome change after a month in the trenches. The 'billets are luxury itself. To sleep in a bed is an entirely new experience for me in France.'

The next day he was writing to Mabel, recalling that it was six weeks to the day since they said goodbye on the station platform. During that time, Bowman had written thirty-three letters to her. He numbered them and kept a note of the sequence.

In early March, he had a series of colds. As soon as he had thrown off one, another developed. Yet however under the weather he felt on 8 March, he fell in when the battalion was on parade for a visit from the Corps Commander, General Haldane. The general spoke flattering words about the fighting quality of Scottish troops; he referred to the coming German offensive and said he was confident that the brigade would be called on to take part in a counter-attack.

The day after the corps commander's visit, Bowman reported sick. He was sent to a field ambulance, 'real bed snowy linen and hot water bottles.' On 11 March he had a high temperature, and the next day he was admitted to the British Red Cross hospital at Le Touquet. It was trench fever. He had been told that its symptoms are similar to those of malaria. It was thought that trench fever was caused by body lice; it could have a debilitating effect on a battalion. A fellow patient, an officer in the Gordon Highlanders, told him that it knocked out practically a whole platoon and laid low ten officers.

While he was in hospital, he wrote daily to Mabel, and he thought about home and family a lot. Would Maisie 'retain any memory of the person behind the "Da-Da" name?' However, he was restless to be declared fit and discharged from hospital: 'I would have been better sooner than I was if they had just left me for 3 days in the field Ambulance.'

Still, it was a case of making the best of it and it gave him a chance to keep up with the latest military thinking. There had been a question mark in his mind over his confidence about 'the new tactics of attack' but now he had completely mastered them. He gave Mabel snippets of war news, and wondered if she had read in the papers about which divisions had been specially mentioned for gallantry. One of them was the 3rd Division: 'Did you notice that another of the three is the 51st? That is the most famous fighting division in the British Army and consists entirely of Highland territorials.' He also kept up with news about political developments back home. There was one area of social policy on which he was particularly keen: educational reform. He told Mabel that he greatly approved of the latest measures to raise the school leaving age that were being proposed in England and Wales: 'Scotland would need to look to its laurels if she is not to be outdistanced by England in educational wisdom.'

In peacetime, the Red Cross Hospital had been a casino that was owned by the Duchess of Westminster. She had given it over to the Red Cross for the duration of hostilities, but she was still living in the area. According to Bowman, one day when there were a lot of admissions, 'the Duchess herself superintended the reception.' On 21 March, he was allowed up and he walked along Le Touquet's promenade Paris-Plage; it had a wide sandy stretch sweeping down to the water. Before the war, it had attracted the rich set on holiday from across the English Channel. An essence of leisure and wealth still hung in the sea air. It was the sort of stroll that could take your mind back to happier days, but in Bowman's case that day, not for long: when he returned to the ward, a nurse told him that a great enemy offensive was under way.

Two days later, the doctor told him he would be discharged from hospital and sent on light duties at the British base, and the next day he was in Étaples and in a large dormitory with other officers. It was here that Bowman learned that the enemy's offensive had broken through part of the allied line.

The war had so far lasted for more than three years: years of carnage and destruction and stalemate. It was widely believed that, in a final attempt, the enemy would launch an offensive in an attempt to drive the British forces back to the coast.

On the evening of 25 March, Bowman wrote his fifty-fifth letter to 'My Own Most Dearly Beloved' who had been in his thoughts a great deal that day:

> I am wondering, my Beloved, how you are bearing up in this hour of greatest strain. But I know, Beloved; I know well. Terrible it is for you, Beloved, terrible in its call for anxious waiting. Yet I know that courage will not fail you – nor cheerfulness – that greatest courage of all – a woman's courage. God will keep you thro' it all – keep you and bless you my Mabel, and restore us to each other in the end – in his good time.

However, Bowman had his fears about the manner in which he might die. He confessed to Mabel that he had a fear of 'being buried alive in a deep dugout which is pounded to pieces by the German artillery or killed in a dugout by gas.'

While he was at the base, he wrote to Kemp Smith from the British Officers' Club. He was worried at the speed of the enemy advance and the fate of the 10/11th HLI, for the 40th Division was in the thick of the fighting and he was impatient to be back with the battalion. He told Kemp Smith that there was only one outcome of the war that would lead to a safe Europe in the future: 'unconditional capitulation is the one formula that satisfies me.' To achieve that the cost might be very high, but in his view, 'if it takes 10 years and all this generation are killed off, futurity will make good all losses, if we remain faithful to our task and finish the job thoroughly.'

> My personal eagerness is splendidly sustained by the backing I get all the time from my wife – no small service. The cost to herself I can divine. The man's share is an easy one indeed. But to wait and suffer and remain invariably cheerful and dole out continual encouragement and stimulus is a sacrifice and service.

As soon as the doctor declared him fit, Bowman reported for service. He drew fresh equipment, a new steel helmet and iron rations. His orders were to take a draft from 'L' camp to the 40th Division. He arrived at the railway station with sixty-two men, and he picked up another draft there for the same division. In all, he had 113 men: some for the 12th Suffolks, the 10/11th HLI, the 14th HLI and 14th Argyll and Sutherland Highlanders. He saw to it that they were issued with blankets and had rations drawn for them for three days. The station was an incredible sight: it was packed with troops; men were sitting anywhere they could find a place to rest; they sat with their backs to the massive wheels of the huge continental locomotives, legs stretched out towards the sleepers of the neighbouring line, not knowing when one of the trains might move off, as gouts of steam issued from the boilers.

At the station, he met two Welsh officers who were on the staff of the 120th Brigade. They told him that the 10/11th HLI 'had done splendidly and had been terribly cut up – more so than the 14th.'

What Bowman returned to with his draft of men was but a tattered remnant of the battalion he had left a few weeks earlier: they had lost 10 officers and 343 other ranks. That remnant of the battalion and the 14th were now absorbed into the 120th Brigade being held in reserve a few miles north-east of Estaires.

On Sunday, 31 March – Easter Sunday – Bowman wrote the sixty-first letter he had sent to Mabel since his arrival in France. He told her that he had gone to a Presbyterian Church service for Highland Regiments 'as it was for the sake of men who were on their way up the line.' It was appropriate for him and, he felt, 'the sermon was most earnest and moving; and thro' it all, my mind was filled with the thoughts of your dear self, with whom I was sharing it all.'

Later that day, Bowman came across Lieutenant McLauchlan, 10/11th HLI, who told him he had been

> spreading the story that I am back at home – which does not please me over much, as it will give capital to the people that used to say: "He'll never stand it." I feel that the toil and hardships are well within my powers of endurance, and that I am even better able to stand them than many an officer and many a man in the ranks.

For the past ten years 1 April had always been a red-letter day to him, and he reminded Mabel of it:

> My own most precious wife,
> Look at the heading of this letter and see what date it is. Eleven years ago this day, my Mabel, that letter was written – the first of how many! – a letter that was to turn the whole tenor of our lives. Can you even think now, my Dearest Love, what our lives might have been if that letter had not been written? And yet at that time you so little realised what was brewing and so little trusted me and your own future that you began in your reply by asking if I was not making an April fool of you.

The next day, he had free time. He walked into Calais to get a haircut, and he had to wait two hours for it. On his way he saw HLI reinforcements marching out. He took the day at a leisurely pace, and went to view Auguste Rodin's famous sculpture 'The Burghers of Calais'. Rodin had completed it a little over twenty years earlier. The sculpture, in the open air, commemorates an event that took place in Calais during the Hundred Years' War, when the town was besieged for a year and its inhabitants were being starved to death. Edward III of England offered to lift the siege if six of the chief citizens surrendered themselves as a sacrifice. Six of them offered themselves up to save the city, in the expectation that they would be killed, and Rodin created expressions of fatalism and acceptance and heroism of self-sacrifice on members of the group.

For Bowman, the sculpture and what it commemorated from a long-distant century back was a sombre reminder of his own position: he was on the point of moving into the line, and he was preparing himself, and Mabel, for the possibility of his death. He wrote to her in terms of what was deepest to him, their love for each other:

> Well, Mabel Dearest, I was uncommonly near you in my dreams last night – in fact I was with you altogether, and it was very sweet. It's so strange, Darling, to have no word from you all these days – no word since the offensive opened, and the great ordeal for you began. I well know, my Dearest, how bravely and cheerfully you are bearing up. Yet I would fain hear it all from you, my Own, your hopes and fears from day to day. How more than thankful I am that you have those dear children! How the dear little things will lighten and sweeten the dark days and nights of waiting! And how even in the darkest hour they will sustain you with the consciousness of a mission and a purpose in life. – O Mabel, I have been thinking in those last days how much you have meant to me – how you have made and remade me, how life for me became a new thing from the moment you first spoke to me. Without you I wonder what I would have been now! Beloved, between those who love, there is no thought of indebtedness, is there – even mutual indebtedness? It is just a question of love and union. And so it is between us. I will not speak of what I owe to you. You have remade my life for me and I have claimed you as my own and given you myself. I am yours, Mabel, as you are mine and nothing can part us. We have tasted the sweetness of uttermost intimacy and life has given us of its best. Let us be strong and endure in the great anguish that love exacts from those who love – remembering the greater blessedness. God watch between us, my Beloved, in these days. The everlasting arms be about you. God bless and save our little ones. Be strong and bright and know that my love watches ever over you and that for ever I am thine own.
>
> Yours, Archie

On Wednesday, 3 April, he wrote a letter to Maisie. He used his written version of infant talk, as though he was sitting speaking to her, and only to her, in a quiet voice; he enclosed three drawings, a bunch of grapes, a rose, and an open-sided train carriage with French soldiers sitting, their feet dangling out:

> This is just a note to your own dear wee self from daddy on the morning of the day when he will be starting to go up to the big battle against the Germans. You know it is for you and our Enie-Bo and our darling Mamming that daddy must go and fight these Germans; because if we did not fight them they would not let us live the way we want to live and to be free men and women. And so you may be sure that is to save you from these Germans that daddy is going to fight them, he is often thinking very fondly of you; and often when he goes to bed at nights he takes out some photographs of you and Enie and our Mamming.

Later that same day Bowman was ordered to proceed with his draft to Divisional HQ and, in sombre mood, he wrote a brief note to Mabel: 'I commit you with infinite tenderness, my Beloved Wife, into God's hands. We shall face the fact calmly together – glozing over nothing.'

The River Lys flows placidly through the city of Estaires; in early April its banks are a delicate green guiding its flow, and Bowman said, in his sixty-sixth letter to Mabel: 'I'd love to give you flowers. Now everything is in the first green and _so_ lovely.' However, a few days later the pastoral scene became a battlefield.

Late on the night of 7 April, General Ludendorff's second offensive began with a ferocious artillery bombardment in the northern sector of the line. This area north of Armentières was held by the Second British Army under General Plumer. South of Armentières was held by the First British Army. The 40th Division, with the 10/11th HLI, was held in reserve. So sustained was the bombardment that it had to be the prelude to a land attack. It went on with high explosives and gas throughout 8 April, but died down in the evening.

The reserve was called upon and the 10/11th HLI, with Bowman in C Company and Captain Cuthbertson in command, moved forward to Nouveau Monde.

From before dawn on the 9th, the attack recommenced and enemy shells were falling on Estaires. At 6.30 am the battalion was ordered to 'Stand to!' just as the cooks arrived from the cookhouse with their large kettles of food for the men. Bowman mentally filed images of the scenes as the battle developed, and just over two weeks later he began writing his account of it and he did it in verse form.

There are strengths in what he did and the way he did it: he wrote it so close to the time it happened that it is free from false memory. Because it is in verse it is concise, taut and the rhythm and images bring out a dramatic quality, putting stress on speed, surprise and the awesome power of heavy artillery. So the narrative that follows comes from Bowman's contemporary account, and contains lines and phrases from his prison camp verses.

The kettles of food arrived, 'but not a man was fed.' They were under orders. 'We mustered, lowering, hungry', but from what point would the attack come? On the ground, it was all part of the spring morning, with banks of mist waiting to be dispersed by sunlight: 'No one dreamed / What menace crouched behind that bankèd mist, / Massing to bear down on us.'

When the first indication came it was from an unexpected quarter. The enemy was already on the north bank of the Lys, and some British troops, men of the Durham Light Infantry, haggard-looking beyond their years, had retreated over a footbridge across the Lys. Their officers were dead, and the position they held was taken by the enemy:

> 'We seek a new position further on.'
> Position! Little recked they then how steep
> The way, how sure the ending. They were gone,
> And the keen harvester prepared to reap
> In fresh fields.

The speed and depth of the enemy's penetration took the allies by surprise, for the enemy was using a new tactic. Instead of sending in waves of infantry to breach the line, the Germans had trained storm troops, and they used them successfully in the first offensive in March. These men were to operate in small detachments, and they were to be the tip of the spear. They picked their way forward in small groups, making use of whatever cover there was such as shell-holes or natural declivities or ditches, all the while under the umbrella of their own artillery and then, as they closed in on a part of the line, their trench mortars. After they had breached the line, the wave of infantry was sent in.

Fresh orders came. The 10/11th HLI was to move to a new position: the church of Nouveau Monde. They ran at the double while shells screamed overhead, but all was deserted on the ground. In between the whine and scream of shells in flight there was an eerie silence with only the sound of their boots on the street, and there they waited:

> Waiting! A soldier's sacrament of strain,
> The eager cup of poising destiny,
> That may not pass from him till it is dry,
> And Death with peace, or Life unveils with pain.

South-east of Nouveau Monde the allied line was held by Portuguese troops of the 2nd Portuguese Division. Under the force of the enemy thrust they fell back in disarray. Those who were not captured left the field. However, the Portuguese green uniform looked rather like the field grey of the German uniform in the morning mist and there was the potential for friendly fire or confusion. A few Portuguese passed through where C Company waited. A Portuguese sergeant reported to them:

> 'Nothing is known of posts that lie before
> Laventie. At the cross-roads hellish fire
> Has cut them off who shouldered the first load.'
> Can they live through it? 'They cannot retire,
> Nor can you reinforce.'

The minutes passed like hours as C Company waited, and that strange capacity of the mind to switch from tense alert to past memories kicked in and Bowman found his thoughts flitting to other settings, to his homeland at this time of year:

> Where April stirs along Loch Lomond side;
> To watch the sands of Morar gently take
> The Atlantic swell that softly combs the Isles;
> And through the gorgeous portals of the Clyde
> To hear at dawn the thudding paddles wake
> The ever-brooding silence of the Kyles.

Suddenly, his reverie was shattered. The heavy artillery had been guided on to fresh targets; shells were landing nearer and nearer. The earth rocked beneath them:

> Men crouched together, shaken as they took
> That presence far too massive for their fear,
> A quivering sense that something tidal welled
> Over their perfect helplessness, and shook
> The core of being; yet that being held.

Then came the order to C Company 10/11th HLI to reinforce the line at Laventie. However, when they got to the shallow breastwork trenches between Nouveau Monde and Laventie, it was too late: there was no line to hold, as it had been breached at heavy cost to the defenders:

> Alas, the lifting battle-fog proclaimed
> The line was gone, with those who bore the brunt,
> Our comrades, whom the fierce Valkyries claimed,
> Closing upon them in the bloody hunt.

Now the tip of the spear was pointing at the position held by C Company. They were low on ammunition and storm troops were moving stealthily, selecting their positions from which to attack. There was an abandoned farm and its outbuildings lining the road:

> Gray figures stealing, and a headlong dash
> From hedge to house, from house again to hedge.
> And fifty rifles levelled on the ledge!
> One instant on the aim, and then, the crash!
> He went to earth and vanished in a flash.

Then came the concentrated machine-gun fire to pin them down:

> We knew the sign, the closing of the net,
> The baying of the pack on every hand,
> Terror of isolation. Still it fanned
> Some flame within. We were not conquered yet.

There was still hope, the hope of reinforcement. However, that was dashed when a sergeant from another company managed to get through to them, running, 'as men run only in the face of death', with the news that north of Laventie had fallen and enemy infantry in columns of four broke through to Estaires. They were trapped. They had fewer than twenty men left and they were almost out of ammunition.

Thus far, as events had turned out for him in his military service, Bowman was untried in battle. Before the day was out, though, he had gained 'absolute confidence in myself as battle-worthy.' However, they could not hold out for long.

The storm troops breached the trench in a brilliant stroke. There were four set moves to it: use of a farm building that gave shelter; then a ditch running alongside a road; a feinted approach from one angle that drew the defenders' fire; a lone storm trooper sprinting 30 yards and getting into position behind them:

> The treacherous shelter of a too-near farm,
> A ditch along a road, a false alarm,
> Thirty yards of the open; in the van
> A desperado running – how he ran! –
> And the pack had us.

By the time the Germans got into the trench, Bowman was unwounded and had already found deep within himself the resolve to fight until they fell or they prevailed. Cuthbertson had a bullet graze to his right forearm and a small piece of shrapnel in his right leg above the ankle, and a tin of cigarettes in his pocket had stopped a bayonet thrust to his stomach. He had done all that a company commander could do, and he gave the order to surrender.

For Bowman, it was the end of serving his country in combat:

> It is the end of all, the bitter end,
> The unpardonable, though ineluctable,
> A breach in life no living now will mend;
> The sin that sinned not; fell not, yet a fall.

The bitter end! It was the nadir of the spirit. He felt as if all the generations of his forefathers who had fought to create the nation he sprang from were gathered, 'Tier after tier upon the banks of time', in judgement on him.

That long, painful march into captivity gave free rein to negative feelings. He had to call upon what he described as 'those lions of thought' to drive them away. Yet even when he succeeded in displacing thoughts of self-blame, there was the reality of what lay ahead for him as a prisoner of war: 'a living death.' Only a few weeks ago his words to Kemp Smith 'if it takes 10 years and all this generation are killed off…' came back. What if, indeed, the war went on for years? Mabel on her own, Ian and Maisie going through the stages of development and starting school, all without knowing him? Bowman had to summon the lions of thought more than once on that long march.

The column of prisoners wound its way south-east, avoiding the main reinforcement routes to the front. All that long first day on the march, the hours dragged out. Sometimes a wounded man would groan aloud. Whoever was nearest him, regardless of rank, would offer encouragement, words of support, some crumb of comfort. However, there was no respite; they had to keep moving south-east along a side-track until out of artillery range.

At least their guards were humane. There was no barking of orders, no prodding with rifle butts to get them moving faster. Rifles slung across their shoulders, they walked alongside the men.

All the unwounded men in the column carried burdens. After weeks in the field, in the trenches, they had developed a soldier's instinct for scrounging whatever helps to make life more comfortable, and they carried their burdens on their backs, in a blanket or in a groundsheet. Some had even prised lengths of duck-boarding from a trench and, like oxen, dragged their load after them.

However, the speed of their advance created resupply problems for the Germans. Horse-drawn wagons had difficulty in keeping up with the pace of the assault due to the nature of the ground, which was soft and waterlogged in places and littered with deep pools. When the prisoners came off the side-tracks they had been following and onto the German supply routes, they had to leave firmer ground and slither about on wet mounds whenever a supply wagon appeared on the firmer ground.

Bowman described a scene in which they had been following tracks made by wheeled vehicles on the firmest ground when a pair of horses yoked to a limber and gun carriage came charging towards the column at full gallop. Startled by the sight of the body of men directly ahead of them, the horses veered away at speed onto softer ground until one of the limber's wheels got bogged down to the axle. The enraged driver stood bracing himself on the limber's crosspiece, cursing and laying on his whip.

The April light was waning, and yet the prisoners trudged on; many were limping. A steady drizzle continued as the column threaded its way south of Laventie and towards the village of Aubers where they were to rest for the night.

Darkness fell. The rumble of artillery to the north-west reverberated, rolling under the low cloud base as the column of men moved slowly, like a legion of the damned on its approach to hell:

> We came to Aubers at the dead of night,
> And found the semblance of that circled hell,
> Which Dante once, damnation's pains to tell,
> Paced out in darkness, agony and fright.

The village had experienced Armageddon. It had been destroyed three years ago in the fighting. Gable ends of buildings stood as a stark symbol to the wrath of the god of war. There was no field ambulance; no medical orderlies to treat the wounded:

> No room was there in stable or in stall,
> Nor roof to shelter cattle while they eat,
> Where wounded men could shelter from the blights
> Of the foul dew that drizzling covered all.
> But in the open and the squelching street
> We left them to endure the drenching night.

On that night in the open and the wet in the ruins of Aubers there was nothing to relieve the pain of the wounded, and of Bowman's company of the 10/11th HLI, he was the 'only man who was sufficiently fit to keep at it and attend to the wounded, as our plight in the open, amidst cold and wet, was truly terrible.'

> Moaning and writhing in their pain they lay;
> And none to turn their faces to the wall,
> And none to close their eyes, and none to pray.

Early in the morning, before dawn, a sudden barrage of howitzers opened up. The next phase of the battle was under way. The prisoners were formed up and ordered to walk. Of this day's march, Bowman wrote that apart from the first phase, this was the bitterest humiliation. However, he acknowledged the kindness of their guards on this gruelling part. The prisoners walked about 12 kilometres that day, hoping and praying that the agony would end. Whatever lay ahead for them could not be any worse, but it turned out to be:

> By Fournes, by Haubourdin, the endless reel
> Of marching men ran out its winding slow,
> Till near day's end, nigh broken on the wheel
> Of hunger, and scarce longer fit to go,
> Within the moated Citadel of Lille
> The sharper pang gave place to deeper woe.

Where they were taken was no prisoner-of-war camp. British troops called it 'the black hole of Lille.' It was Le Fort de Mons, one of a line of forts built by the French as a defensive line after the Franco-Prussian War of 1870, and the Germans used it as a holding camp for their prisoners until they could transport them to prisoner-of-war camps. Conditions were appalling: very little light, overcrowding, insanitary conditions, dysentery and no medical support.

Bowman described only his feelings when the locks were turned and bolts shot home:

> And next a settling helplessness appals
> The sinking soul, as if that hour should blot
> One's name out of the Book, as if one caught
> Of life's retreat the hurrying last footfalls.

Chapter Three

Behind Toothed Wire

Within these cages day by day we pace
The bitter shortness of the meted span;
And this and that way variously we plan
Our poor excursions over the poor place,
Cribbed to extinction. Yet remains one grace.

A.A. Bowman,
Sonnets from a Prison Camp

Through the high barbed-wire fence of *Offizier-Kriegsgefangenenlager* Rastatt, Bowman watched the distant wooded slopes of the Black Forest, gilded with evening sunlight:

   Wistful eyes
Wandered from peak to peak, as if to sound
Their mystery, if perchance there might be found
Some healing essence there, some glad surprise.

The voice in the poem was searching for a presence Bowman last sensed, years before, in Scotland, walking in Glendaruel on a May morning: a sense of the divine in nature, something akin to Wordsworth's insight 'there is a spirit in the woods.' Patiently the watcher stood, scanning the pine-clad heights, 'When suddenly – the mystic rune was learned!'

Whatever the rune revealed, it was here, in a prisoner-of-war camp within sight of the Black Forest that Bowman began to undergo a powerful personal development.

When he was captured, he assumed that prison camp would be 'a living death.' However, it turned out to be quite the opposite! It was a transformative experience; he discovered the range of his teaching gifts and his potential to make an impact far beyond the world of academe. His friend and colleague Norman Kemp Smith said of him: 'He came out of the [Prison] Camps with an assurance of gifts and powers, and of possibilities of their use, which he had never before allowed himself to recognise.'

For a few days Bowman endured the misery of Le Fort de Mons, 'the black hole of Lille', before he was taken by train to the officers' prisoner-of-war camp at Rastatt in Baden-Baden. It was a transit prison camp where prisoners were held until they were sent to permanent camps.

Prisoners of war in Germany were treated in accordance with the Hague Conventions: they had shelter from the elements and they were fed, albeit on poor and inadequate food, but, by April 1918, the German population was no better off than the prisoners.

Bowman's first priority was to write to Mabel. Gone were the days of writing a letter almost daily. On 16 April 1918, he wrote on the small official prisoner-of-war card, 14cm x 9cm, 'Most Dearly Beloved, Your agony has come; but this will end it. I am in the best of health & all is well. God bless you and keep you until we meet again!' He told her that he was allowed to write only three letter-cards and four postcards a month on officially-issued stationery, but there was no restriction on the number of letters he could receive. He also managed to squeeze in the message: 'I am sending a PC to arrange for your maintenance with McGrigor.' The shorthand here referred to Sir Charles R. McGrigor, one of the three firms of army agents and bankers that were used by some regiments as an alternative to the army paymaster for distributing officers' pay. Bowman told Mabel to send him nothing until she heard from him again: 'I get 60 M. per month for food etc. & am not allowed more.'

When he handed that official card over to the prison authorities, it was the start of a long process for a prisoner of war's mail: it went first to the German censor to be scrutinized; then it passed into the mailing system of a neutral country, Denmark; and the whole process took weeks or even months before it arrived at a prisoner's home. Every centimetre of paper or card and letter-card was space for writing; there were no indentations for new paragraphs and the ampersand sign took up less space than the conjunction 'and'.

The next day, 17 April, Bowman wrote to Mabel again, using the first of his three letter-cards for the month:

> To my Most Dearly Beloved Wife,
> Mabel, I went through the first terrible phase of the Battle of the Lys. Of my experiences there I cannot write at length, but will tell you this. We lay for 10 hours under terrible fire before the infantry attack arrived. We were hopelessly outnumbered, surrounded by a ring of machine-gun fire & finally bombed out of our position. My vote was cast for a fight to the finish, but Mr Cuthbertson who was in command ordered the surrender. I do not blame him. He is a splendid fellow & was wounded in two places. But to me the act of surrender was almost unendurable.

When he went on to talk about the wounded, the German censor obliterated first one sentence and then a whole section. Bowman would learn from experience over the next two months which subjects to avoid, for in some cases the censor prevented the letter entering the system.

Where he was on safe ground was in restricting himself to his needs and his wishes. His first card, compressing the maximum amount of information about himself, expressions of love for his family and requests for items of clothing and toiletries, was written on 23 April:

> <u>Dearest</u>, Do you <u>know</u> yet? I <u>yearn</u> to hear. Am in <u>perfect</u> health. <u>Every trace</u> of fever gone. Have <u>no anxiety</u>. Write how you stand financially, civil liabilities, children's allowances etc. Could you send one waterproof, 3 handkerchiefs, set underwear (sox), hat (civilian), 3 khaki collars, *Dombey & Son*, *The Scarlet Letter*, pr. gloves, 1piece of soap, tube tooth paste & hard brush, tin Heinz's baked beans. All parcels thro' Red X. Consult post-office. Tenderest love to children. Thinking of Eenie's [Ian's] birthday. Dear love to Mother, Mrs Stewart, Alick, Johnnie & your father. All at home aunts. Reassure everybody. Myself <u>very</u> fit, resolute & <u>cheerful</u>. – To yourself, Mabel, love unspeakable & everlasting – sweetest memories & brightest hopes. Yours for this life & forever.
>
> Archie X X X

When it came to creature comforts, life in a prisoner-of-war camp was primitive: he had what he stood up in when he was captured; he had no coat, he had no change of clothing for the best part of a month, no razor or hand-mirror. To obtain them he was reduced to a child-like dependency. Yet a prison camp was also where a man's strength of spirit could emerge. Until 9 April he had been untested in battle, but on that day he discovered he was battle-worthy. Now, as a prisoner of war, bereft of even the most basic of life's requirements, he came into his own as an intellectual and a moral force with a contribution to make to the wider community. Years later, in his notes for a talk to a lay audience, he defined morale as the balance of spirit over circumstance. It was here, in the grim conditions of the prison camps, that Bowman, in Norman Kemp Smith's words, 'came to his full stature, as the man that imposed himself, as by natural right, and made so deep an impression on the Princeton community in the years 1919 to 1926, and on the University and City of Glasgow in the last 10 years of his life.'

Up until now, Bowman's work in education had been entirely in the academic world. Certainly he had a training remit in the army but that was instruction, as per regulations, in skills and practice, not education with the aim of opening the mind and encouraging thinking. Yet even in a prison camp, he took the initiative and gave himself an educational role, and he did it without the support of textbooks or the back-up of prepared lecture notes. He found the inner resources and strength of personality to hold the attention of large numbers of mixed-ability learners. Also, in addition to the subjects he described in this first detailed letter of daily life he sent to Mabel, he added courses on philosophy and psychology. Then on top of the educational role, he accepted a range of responsibilities that did not accrue to his military rank but to his knowledge and self-presentation.

What was apparent from the work schedule he gave himself in Rastatt, and became a characteristic of him throughout his life, was that when he gave of himself, he did it without stint:

My Most Dearly Beloved,

If I only were sure that you knew by now that I am alive & well, I'd be positively happy. I long to hear from you & to know, Dear Heart, that the agony of your suspense is over. How much more awful it is for you than for me. Neither the battle nor the horrors of the succeeding night nor the imprisonment that now holds me can approach the sum of your sufferings. But the dawn must be at hand my Love, & I know that God's blessing has followed you all the way in your darkest journey. – I am in absolute topping form, & though a prisoner, am as busy as the day is long. Ever since I was taken I have acted as interpreter and intermediary between the English officers & the German authorities, & in that capacity I have a great deal to do here – e.g. to attend in the canteen while the day's purchases are being arranged between the English & German authorities, to attend at all issues of pay, translate all complaints & explain all the points that arise as to rates etc., to interview the General from time to time (I was summoned by him today), & generally speaking to help everybody who has any difficulty. I am also chief lecturer to the camp. The demands on me for lectures are simply enormous, & the appreciation of the men almost pathetic. They waylay me night and day with entreaties & offerings of thanks. I even get presents of food. Have lectured on Russia and Germany & twice on America, & practically everybody turns out to hear. I am also newspaper-translator, general authority for referring all such questions as the possible duration of the war. And when you consider that in our compound alone there are 600 to 700 officers all mixed up together behind barbed wire you can understand that my position here is no sinecure. But it is a joy to be able to do something for my comrades. Alas! All the HLI leave for their permanent camps on Monday, & I am being left behind – why, I do not know. The German authorities treat me with every mark of respect and courtesy, & probably they wish to use me a little longer here. Among the prisoners there are a fair number of charming Americans, & they have been most friendly.

The censor then obliterated the next three lines.

Concern for Mabel had been Bowman's first priority, that she should know he was alive and that she should have enough funds; then he took on a teaching commitment to be of service to his comrades, and then he turned his hand to the third activity, which was for himself. He had a notebook on him when he was captured and he began to write a series of poems in sonnet form, beginning with the battle at the Lys. When he was satisfied with each one, he dated it. He completed the first three on 27 April. He was fired up; a sense of urgency comes through. He wrote sixteen sonnets under the heading 'In the Field' between 27 April and 1 May; then he wrote two for a group he called 'The Nadir'; then between 2 and 5 May he wrote eight for the group 'On the March', which ended as the prisoners arrived at Lille.

Then, on 7 May, he began what would become four on a new topic, 'Rastatt', in which the mood changes:

> Within these cages day by day we pace
> The bitter shortness of the meted span;
> And this and that way variously we plan
> Our poor excursions over the poor place,
> Cribbed to extinction.

In all, in the course of thirteen days, he wrote thirty-six sonnets.

At the start of his allocation of mail for the month of May, he wrote to Mabel:

> Most Dearly Beloved, Another week has gone & I am in high hope that the awful period of your suspense is over. My thoughts are continually with you & my soul yearns & hungers over you every night in prayer. Fond, too, are my thoughts of all my dear ones. Ere this reaches you with its burden of love, our little Eenie [Ian] will have passed his 3rd birthday. A father's blessings on his little ones!

Before he used up all the space on the official letter, he asked for a book: Wordsworth or Hardy's *Return of the Native* or Chaucer (with glossary), Shakespeare or Turgenev (*Rudin*, *Virgin Soil*).

Bowman had admiration for the Anglican chaplains; he told Mabel that 'the Anglican padres are magnificent, and the camp has developed an amazing religious life.' There were services every night, and Bowman made a good friend of the

Anglican chaplain the Reverend Arthur Karney, whom he described as a charming and saintly man who hoped to come out and visit them in Princeton after the war.

At the beginning of May, a new camp commandant took over command of Rastatt prison. As far as the prisoners were concerned, the first noteworthy thing about the changeover was an improvement in their food. However, that was followed by what seemed to be a tightening of the management regime: the German authorities no longer allowed the prisoners to have German newspapers and foreign newspapers were also forbidden.

It was just another imposed condition that had to be lived with. Bowman, in one of his letters, asked Mabel to write to Kemp Smith and say that the latter should tell Macneile Dixon 'one does not dream what love of country can become until one is a prisoner in a strange land, & that the very thought of Shakespeare one day brought a lump to my throat.' He also asked her to say to Kemp Smith that 'my soul is triple steel against adversity & that no matter what the future holds I shall neither bend nor break.'

However, his nagging worry was whether Mabel had enough money to live on. He did not know the regulations governing a prisoner of war's pay, and whether additional allowances were paid on top of his army pay. He wrote: 'My pay is 11/6 per day. Should Civil Allowance Liabilities for insurance be stopped, borrow from N. K. [Norman Kemp Smith] on security of my policy.' He withdrew £10 via the agency on the camp – 'I hated to do it' – and thought it would keep him going indefinitely. He hoped, though, that when he got to his permanent camp he would be able to draw a little money from Berlin which, he learned, he could do by special arrangement.

From what he heard from other prisoners, Bowman knew by now that it could be weeks ahead before he heard from Mabel. Some prisoners had already been there eight weeks and had yet to receive a letter. The last letter he had from Mabel was when he left hospital at Le Touquet.

***

Mabel, for her part, had her work cut out. She had supported her husband when he felt his duty was to leave Princeton to fight for his country, and she was now left bringing up their two young children in the Stewart family home. Her father was in poor health and needed a lot of nursing, and her mother was becoming less able to do it. Her brother Johnnie was single; he worked in Glasgow and No. 77 Montgomerie Street was still his home. The family employed a servant, but Mabel had a poor opinion of her worth; she felt she was slovenly.

Ian and Maisie had their share of the usual childhood illnesses. However, in the spring, Ian developed mucus colitis and they had to call in a doctor.

Throughout, Mabel coped very well. According to Bowman's sister Daisy, Mabel was 'a perfect hero.'

Her friend Jennie was very much part of her life in 1918. Jennie was now Jennie Mackay; she had married Harry, whom Mabel had invited to join them at Leven when Archie was a training officer. Mabel's match-making seems to have contributed to the marriage, for a week after Jennie's mother died, she wrote to Mabel: 'You will know that Harry Mackay was with us for the week-end. He was a great comfort, Mabel. I am going to marry him some day dearie. I expect you would guess as much.' Now she was pregnant with the baby due in August, and she loved coming round and spending time with Ian and Maisie. She had gone through an anxious time when the newspapers were reporting on the enemy spring offensive in late March because Harry was in the 14th HLI which was part of the 40th Division that was in the thick of the fighting.

On Friday, 5 April, late in the evening, Mabel began writing a letter to Archie. She had missed a deadline she had given herself the previous evening to write to him after the children were asleep because 'I was so tired that I thought the best thing would be to go to bed.' She had hardly got under way with her letter before she had second thoughts: 'I doubt I'll not get writing tonight for Ian is simply hollering.' She had tried writing earlier but

> Ian wakened up and wakened Maisie. Then came Aunt Mina and there was nothing for it but to have both the children up. Maisie seems to have settled but Ian is still crying. Poor wee chap he is not himself yet. Dr Anderson says it will be a while before he is.

At that point, she had to give up the attempt and attend to Ian.

Next morning, when she took up her pen, the mail had just arrived. The army postal service taking the forces' mail from France to the UK was impressively efficient. Bowman's letter from Estaires, enclosing the two letters he had written to Maisie and Ian, was in Mabel's hands:

> Dearest, word has just come in that you are once more on your way up the line. The children's letters made me so very sad, dearest. I think they are perfectly beautiful letters and whatever may be, these letters will be kept as treasures. I'll read Ian his just now and then put it away for him to get with the others later on. <u>Dear</u>, dear heart, I know how terrible it is for you to be parted from us, from me and the dear children. They are such a comfort and joy to me and it really does help make things more bearable to have one's time occupied day and night. God bless you my Archie in what lies before you and may He keep you safe and bring you back to us. The

lists are coming out now and alas many, many will be the sore hearts in this country of ours. I see that Jean Ingram has lost her husband. He was in the Royal Engineers. I used to know her long ago… and lately I met her again in Jennie's. She was looking forward to taking up home in Montreal after the war and was interested in hearing that I had been there… I feel that we have had eleven years of life since that early 1st of April. We have, haven't we, my beloved but we'll be glad to have more and even more. I am so sorry for those who have had just a short fleeting married life – snatched between periods of service. I think I'm sorriest though for the young lads who have fallen just as they were bursting into manhood.

A few days later, such a young lad's death came closer to home. Her brother, Johnnie, came in with a black-edged envelope, 'and said quite quietly that Jamie had been killed. Jamie is the boy Cochrane of the dear Loch Fyne days for whom Johnnie has always had such a great affection.' Jamie had been in the Stewart home the year before and spent the day with Johnnie:

He was on leave from the front. His father died very suddenly and Jamie got leave to come home for the funeral. He was too late for that but was there to console his mother in her grief. Now he, her only son, has gone too. She wrote such a beautiful brave letter to Johnnie telling him that her beloved son and his dear friend, Jamie, had been killed in action. It is so very sad my dearest love what sorrow these last few weeks must have brought to millions. Yet always one feels it is the only way and however bitter, the cup must be drunk.

Women who lost a son or a husband in the war had to find the strength to endure. There were no symbols or funeral rituals to bring any sense of closure. In his poem *Anthem for Doomed Youth*, Wilfred Owen touches on the lingering sorrow in the now lonely home to which only memories return: 'Their flowers the tenderness of patient minds, / And each slow dusk a drawing down of blinds.'

Each morning, and right through the day until the evening, when it was often most difficult, Mabel tried to be optimistic. 'I am trying to keep as cheerful and hopeful as possible,' Mabel wrote, knowing that Archie was in the line, 'and you are not to let the thought of me worry you in the least.' Yet while she tried hard not to be anxious for him, she worried: 'I think and think of you in danger and hope and pray that you may be spared.'

On 11 April the newspapers were full of the news of the latest enemy offensive. Mabel had been busy with the children and it was evening before she had time to write to Archie:

My beloved Archie

I looked at the [*Glasgow*] *Herald* and found the papers ringing with the new offensive on the Lys. Beloved, I am like thousands of other women in this country, waiting to hear what has happened to their dearest ones. I am hoping with all my soul that you are safe, yet I know that even if I escape there are others who will quiver under the blow. Jennie was here tonight. She came round with Cathie and her young cousin. Harry too is near you and together we felt the anxiety that so many are feeling. I felt sorrier for Jennie than for myself as she has had all the strain of the Arras time to be up against and now with only a few days' remission the strain begins again. Jennie is less able just now to bear anxiety and she has more time to think things than I have.

Over the next two days, the newspaper headlines were alarmist and Mabel wrote:

My Beloved

I don't know what to think. I look at the map to see Estaires well inside the German lines and I wonder what has happened to my dearest and where he is. I am not impatient beloved for I know it may be days or weeks before I hear but I long to know. The situation seems to grow graver every day. This seems to be a bad push they are making, a strong bid for the Channel ports. The Armentières business seems to have been a pretty bad one. Evidently the Germans surrounded the place, gassed out the whole garrison. I am afraid of the gas for you dearest. I think it may affect you worse than most people yet I must just wait with patience and hope. This must only be a line dearest. I couldn't get writing last night. Both children wakened up completely just when I was going to begin, Maisie crying lustily so there was nothing for it but to go to bed with them. Five of the club girls came round last night and they were all pretty charmed with Maisie in particular.

While she was writing, Ian told her he wanted to write to his daddy. 'I asked him what would he write. "Two kisses." I said, do them yourself. "But little boys need their mammies to help them write to their daddies when their daddies are in France."'

Then, three days later, for reasons she could not explain, Mabel's fears for Archie departed, and in a remarkable coincidence of dates, on 16 April she wrote to him on the same day that he was writing his first card to her from Rastatt: 'Since yesterday dearest I've been strangely easy in my mind about you. I feel that whatever is to happen has happened by this time and if you are safe you are probably out of it and resting for a bit.'

Mabel's strange feeling that a shadow had passed her husband by stayed with her, but it would take a few weeks before she heard anything about him. What she then heard at first turned out to be false, for, in the fog of war, by the end of the first day of the Battle of the Lys, another version of what happened to Bowman was forming in his battalion.

At around 11.00 pm on 9 April, as Bowman and his fellow prisoners were exposed to the elements, huddled like cattle in the ruins of Aubers, what was left of the 10/11th and 14th HLI retreated across the River Lys. They gathered at Le Petit Mortier. Captain Harry Mackay of the 14th HLI came across Captain J.F. Marshall, the adjutant of the 10/11th HLI, when both of them were foraging around for somewhere to rest. They found an abandoned house and sheltered there for a couple of hours.

In their assessment of how the day had gone, Mackay asked Marshall if he knew how Archie Bowman had fared. 'Oh Bowman got a blighty one and got away all right.' The term 'a blighty one' was army jargon for a wound that meant you would be returned to the UK for treatment. Mackay asked him if he was sure of it. 'Yes, he got down the line all right,' Marshall said. Mackay later had this confirmed by Lieutenant McLauchlan, who told him that Bowman had gone in the last Red Cross wagon 'to cross the bridge over the Lys before it was shelled to bits.'

When the cadre of both battalions was withdrawn from the line, Harry Mackay wrote to his wife, Jennie, to assure her he was safe, and he mentioned what he had been told about Bowman so that she could tell Mabel, lest Bowman be unable to write to her from hospital.

Mabel then wrote to Lieutenant McLauchlan's wife to see if her husband had told her anything about Archie, but there was nothing to go on from her reply:

> John saw the battalion or what was left of it on their return and I'm sure you may take it as genuine that your husband isn't badly wounded. I hope however that he gets home to you but he is so conscientious it would be like him to refuse. He is really very good & I don't wonder you are anxious.

By the third week of April, though, Mabel still had only anecdotal reports about her husband. She then wrote to Harry Mackay in the hope that he could tell her whether Archie was in France or the UK and whether he was badly wounded. She also wrote to Norman Kemp Smith asking if he could find out through the Ministry of Information.

Mabel's letter arrived at Kemp Smith's office on 22 April. He acted on it right away and replied to Mabel that same day:

> I have been very anxious to have news of Archie in those critical days. You have, as you must know, my heartfelt sympathy in the anxious waiting for further word. When your letter arrived this afternoon, a major working at the War Office happened to be with me, and he offered to make all possible enquiries… even if he is in German hands – that would at least keep him safe till the end of the war.

Three days later, on 25 April, Mabel received a telegram from the commanding officer of the 10/11th HLI consisting of a single sentence: 'Lt Bowman wounded 9/4/18.' On the same day she got a letter from Norman Kemp Smith, who now had contacts in the War Office:

> I called at War Office and found that a personal call elicited more information than had been obtained by my Major friend. It seems that a cable was sent you on April 19th to New Jersey by the WO stating that Archie was wounded on April 9th (<u>no</u> information as to nature of wound). Since the 19th no further word has reached the WO regarding Archie. I saw the officer in charge, and he said this was a case for special enquiry, and that such special enquiry would be initiated at once. He added that usually when so many days elapse, after the date of wounding, without notification of arrival in one of our hospitals, the explanation is that the wounded man is a prisoner. Any information that comes will be sent you at once, and to your <u>Glasgow</u> address, which I gave him.

So now doubt was introduced, and it was soon to be reinforced for Mabel.

The army postal service delivered Mabel's letter to Harry Mackay on 27 April, and he replied to her with more details of what he had been told. He also added a caveat in the form of a postscript: 'PS. McLauchlan wasn't in the battle, but is quoting a sergeant who said that the wagon was the last one to cross the bridge over the Lys before it was shelled to bits. Still once over the river it was all right.'

Kemp Smith's further efforts yielded results, and on 2 May he sent a telegram to Mabel: 'Good news, Archie a prisoner and in good health. War Office received information last night from British Red Cross Copenhagen. Burman telegram was a mistake.'

Then Kemp Smith followed it up with a letter that explained the cryptic last sentence. He had advised Mabel to write to the Casualty Section, and someone there misread her signature as 'Burman', which, they said, was the name of a

South African in the Rifle Brigade who had been wounded on 9 April. Kemp Smith added a comment here: 'Evidently the supervision of this part of the WO work is very defective.'

Finally, however, Mabel received a formula telegram from the War Office: 'The Military Secretary is desired by the Secretary of State for War to congratulate Mrs Bowman on the safety of her husband.'

In the meantime, however, a compound of two versions of what happened to Bowman crossed the Atlantic, and on 13 May the *New York Times* ran an article on Bowman. Someone at Princeton arranged for a newspaper-cutting bureau to send a copy of it to Mabel. The agency was called Henry Romeike. Above the owner's name, in smaller font, was the slogan, taken from lines by Robert Burns – 'O wad some power the giftie gie us / To see oursels as ithers see us' – and the address was 106-110 Seventh Avenue, New York. The blurb described it as 'The First Established and Most Complete Newspaper-Cutting Bureau in the World.'

> Prof Bowman Missing
>
> Former Princeton Professor May be a Prisoner in Germany
>
> Professor Archibald A. Bowman, formerly head of the Department of Philosophy at Princeton University, has been reported missing at the front in France. From reports received by President Hibben it is learned that Professor Bowman was wounded in the early days of the drive. He was removed to a hospital a short distance behind the front lines, and in the rapid advance of the Germans the hospital was captured. He is now reported by the British War Office as missing, and grave fears are entertained for his safety, as his wound is said to have been serious.
>
> Professor Bowman came here in 1912 as Professor of Philosophy. He returned to England in 1915 to enter the service of his country. Having already had some military training, he was held for a considerable time in England as an instructor in an officers' training school.
>
> In 1914 and 1915, while he was still at Princeton, he was frequently seen practicing signalling with his colleague Dr Glover, who received the DSO for his conduct during the Somme offensive and is still with the British forces in France.
>
> Professor Kemp Smith, another member of the Department of Philosophy, is now serving England.

Mabel still had to wait until 23 May to get her husband's first prisoner-of-war card, the card he had written on 16 April. She wrote to him right away: 'My best beloved, At last I have heard from you and I'm so thankful. Were you wounded, my dearest? I think you must have been but only the wound was not a serious one.' She told him of her fears in the early days when she had no idea about what had happened to him:

> It was indeed a strain when I couldn't be sure what had happened to you but my own instinct was you were safe without much to go on. I was very anxious all the Tuesday and Wednesday, but on the Wednesday night I felt relief from anxiety. Kemp Smith was the dear and true friend that you know him to be and did all in his power to get information for me. It was from him first that I heard you were a prisoner.

She told Archie about the children, and about Ian's illness: 'however, the little fellow is quite his old self again and as cheery as ever. As for Maisie, she runs about everywhere as fast as anything and is very sweet and fascinating.'

Her mind now at ease, Mabel wrote letter after letter to him, knowing each one would take weeks to reach him. At first she had concerns about his likely state of mind now that he was a prisoner: 'I know the bitterness of this separation will eat deep into your soul'; or over against her fears for him, giving him encouragement: 'I keep thinking of Dostoyevsky and how his confinement only enriched his experience.'

In all her letters, she gave Bowman glimpses of the children's development:

> Maisie is the dearest, light-footed little creature, full of mischievousness and warming ways and a great friend and chum of big Eenie Bo. They play together wonderfully now and are so jolly and happy. As for the little man, he too is getting along very well and is recovering from the attack of mucus colitis he had some months ago.

In early June, she took the children to the Botanic Gardens where the hawthorn trees were laden with blossom and fragrant although it had passed its best. The children ran wild, like young animals: 'Maisie was off like a shot when I laid her down and was running into all sorts of forbidden places with Ian encouraging her.'

On 4 June, Mabel received a copy of a letter that Captain Robert Cuthbertson sent to his father 'in which he makes very friendly mention of you.'

Cuthbertson had commanded C Company when they were captured, and at Rastatt, before Cuthbertson left with all the HLI prisoners bar Bowman, they exchanged their Glasgow addresses. Cuthbertson was taken first to Karlsruhe, and ended up at his permanent camp at Mainz. In his first letter home to his parents, he gave them Mabel's address:

An HLI Lieut was caught with me – an awfully nice chap – he was a professor in an American university. He joined the 10/11th HLI in January and proved himself a brave soldier. Nessie might call on his wife at 77 Montgomerie Street N. Kelvinside (just over the Kirklee Bridge) Mrs A A Bowman. Lieut Bowman is here in Germany. Mrs Bowman may call at '41' some day. She has two kiddies. Bowman is writing to her saying you may call. Mrs Bowman was a university graduate.

At long last, on 13 June, eight weeks after he wrote it, Mabel received Archie's first letter:

My most dearly loved Archie

I got your letter card written from Baden on 17th April when I returned from Edinburgh this morning. It has taken a long time to come but it has brought me great joy and comfort. It has brought more than me that for I sent it round to Sutherland Terrace [where Bowman's mother lived] at once and they were all glad to have a reading of it. Oh my dear, dear love, I can feel for you so entirely. I could have wept to think what surrender must have meant to your brave spirit but since the first word came that you were a prisoner I knew you would accept your lot as cheerfully as you could and make the best of it. We miss you terribly here dear heart. I feel my mind so dull and stagnant for poor little Eenie compared with yours but I too am cheerful dear and will wait with the patience that you taught me for our reunion.

Tell me as much as you can of yourself. Have you many pupils for German and what sort of teacher do you make? I suppose your philosophy lectures are general and rather elementary, much like the ones I used to listen to.

I say dear, were you really not wounded at all? The report that I got was that you were. You should see the lovely paragraph that appeared in the *New York Times* about you – Princeton Professor Missing with the usual padding that Americans put in. Dr Glover and Professor Kemp Smith sort of figure in it – sort of secondary stars.

A few months earlier, however, Kemp Smith had the star role when his book *A Commentary to Kant's Critique of Pure Reason* was published. It was well received, being favourably reviewed in the journal *The Nation* by Bertrand Russell, who wrote: 'Professor Norman Kemp Smith's work is admirably done. He is an affectionate but not undiscriminating admirer of Kant's work, a very careful student not only of Kant but of his predecessors… Kemp Smith's book is a much-needed addition to

British Kant-Literature.' Professor G. Dawes Hicks, reviewing it for the academic journal *Mind*, said: 'The work is that of a genuine thinker.'

***

At *Offizier-Kriegsgefangenenlager* Rastatt, on 12 May it became Bowman's turn to be transferred to a permanent camp. He was given no warning about its being imminent, but simply given the order. He just had time to 'shove my belongings into my pockets and go.'

Then came the blow: his poems were confiscated. However, they were not military papers and according to the Hague Conventions a prisoner of war's personal belongings were to remain his property. Nevertheless, the new commandant may have been watching his back: there could be repercussions at *Kommandantur* level for allowing written material referring to recent military operations to be released beyond the camp. The only concession Bowman got was that the verses would not be destroyed; they would remain with the camp authorities.

Chapter Four

Prison Camp Lines

It ought to be a pleasure to acknowledge generosity in an enemy; and I wish to express my indebtedness to Captain Hohnholz, Commandant of the Prison-Camp at Hesepe, to whose kindness I owe it that I am able to offer the sonnets as they stand for publication.

Offizier-Gefangenenlager
Hesepe, 17 August 1918
A.A. Bowman, Foreword to *Sonnets from a Prison Camp*

The prisoners were marched through the great fortress of Rastatt on their way from the prison camp to the railway station. There were magnificent chestnut trees in the courtyard, 'simply loaded with the most gorgeous blossom, white and red.' Bowman later captured the scene in a poem *The Chestnuts* (see Appendix II).

In wartime Germany, a train carrying prisoners of war had no priority status when it came to timetabling. It was a two-day journey northward, and a strange experience. From the carriage windows it was as though, at some junction, the points had switched the train on to a line taking them back in time. There were no shell-pocked ruined buildings and the land had not been ravaged by clashing armies, but the land was not being worked; though early in the evening, they might have seen a woman leading two working horses to the farm stable, and when they passed through stations it was older railwaymen who were on duty.

During that journey, Bowman wondered if he would ever see his poems again. It was wartime, and all he had was the word of an enemy. He dearly wanted to have them. He had put a lot of himself into them, he had proved himself in battle, and had to accept the humiliation of surrender, so he wrote for therapy, a balm to the soul: 'it was a labour that "stood between my soul and madness."'

He wrote his poems in the Petrarchan sonnet form – the fourteen-line poem, with its strict rhyme scheme, focusing on a theme, divided into octave and sestet – which suited his purpose and his cast of mind. Eventually the war would end and men would write their memoirs, but he wanted to express his feelings as the battle went through its stages: the movement, the noise and the range of emotions he experienced, from warrior aggression to child-like shame and despair. Poetry was the medium he chose with its rhythm and richness of connotations, and he kept the poems free from military jargon and the sort of tactical or strategic digressions to which a prose account would be prone. Certainly, for the most part, in the battle sequence and the march to captivity, it works well.

As he was crafting those thirty-six poems, it occurred to him that they might be worthy of publication. There was a flow to them. He had created an action sequence of a major battle, from heavy bombardment to the ground-attack in cinematic terms.

In the first three sonnets he deals with the artillery prelude to the ground movement that would follow. Then he chooses the scenario of a river cutting through a battlefield where, from C Company's position, the action is still unseen: there is a bridge and some fighting men appear on it; a setting for confusion.

For his fourth sonnet, Bowman takes the theme of a footbridge which Durham Light Infantry survivors – from a position that bore the brunt of the first wave of the attack – manage to reach and cross: they are disoriented, but they are still disciplined soldiers looking for another command, and all the while, as his company waits, the Grim Reaper cuts swathes with his scythe:

> IV
> The bridge across the Lys! A slender thread
> To bind or bar thy holders to their own;
> But one span, small and narrow, lightly thrown
> Over these sullen waters, lightly shed.
> Upon thy planks the heavy-booted tread
> Of men who seemed with sudden trouble grown
> Haggard. 'What are you?' 'Durhams.' 'What is known?'
> 'Our billet down, our officers are dead.
> We seek a new position further on.'
> Position! Little recked they then how steep
> The way, how sure the ending. They were gone,
> And the keen harvester prepared to reap
> In fresh fields. The mourne blanket of the dawn
> Gathered the Durhams to eternal sleep.
>
> Rastatt, 28 April

Then, when it came to the encirclement of C Company, Bowman linked two sonnets:

XIII

Gray figures stealing, and a headlong dash
From hedge to house, from house again to hedge,
   And fifty rifles levelled on the ledge!
  One instant on the aim, and then, the crash!
   He went to earth, and vanished in a flash.
And there once more was house, and there was hedge,
With sprouting field, and farm, and ditch with sedge,
   And crop-head pollard row and leafless ash –
  A cheerless landscape gray, and the profound
   Loneliness of the battlefield. The next
Moment trench-mortar shells were on our head;
   Another, and the day was sealed and fixed
On front and flank. Among the stricken dead,
One in the skull, behind, his summons found.

Rastatt, 1 May

XIV

– Found it behind, while yet his soul was set
And his eyes eager with the death he planned
For his foe forward, where he stood and manned
   His gun upon the roaring parapet.
  We knew the sign, the closing of the net,
   The baying of the pack on every hand,
   Terror of isolation. Still it fanned
Some flame within. We were not conquered yet.
  Circled with unseen fire, we only heard
   The bullets whistle round us, only saw
   The solitude of battle. Nothing stirred.
  And yet, unseen, we felt his forces draw
Upon us, earthed at length where earth had lured
   Treacherously to cover. We endured.

Rastatt, 1 May

In what had been an intense burst of creative energy, he went on to describe the aftermath, the forced march to Lille's old fortress. Then he wrote another ten about his experiences at Rastatt, but all that work was left behind at Rastatt.

It was now a month since Bowman had been captured, the train was taking the prisoners further from the front, and the war was receding into the background. However, when they got to their new camp at Hesepe, Westphalia, he began writing again and this time about Hesepe. It was a much smaller camp, and set in attractive countryside:

> I
> A lonely camp and small amidst the miles
> Of the Westphalian plain, where islanded
> In the green waste our simple lives are led
> Out of the troubled world. Here morning smiles
> Splendidly, and the mustering twilight wiles
> To a strange sense of peace consummated
> Over these low-hung woods, where setting red
> And oval the sun the yearning eye beguiles.
> Then as the white and sheeted vapour steals
> Along the flats lagoon-like, comes a breath
> Of anguish from the void, where still is hurled
> Nation on nation; and the spirit feels
> A tidal presence of o'erwhelming death
> Stir through this weird backwater of the world.
>
> Hesepe, 19 May

In this collection there are much larger gaps between the finished poems: he entitled a new group *Hesepe* and dated the first of them 19 May, but the second of them was written eleven days later:

> II
> How hard it is to think upon this shoal
> Of inanition that the world's ablaze.
> How hard to link these lazy summer days
> With ends and issues that will not unroll
> Their length in aeons – mankind's furthest goal,
> Perpending in the thick and murderous haze
> Of yonder battle-hurricane that lays
> Legions to rest till the last tattoo roll.
> On sun-beat sand the busy ants deploy;
> Industrious spiders ply their little looms;
> With brush and pencil or with book we toy.
> The quiet evening nears; the beetle booms.
> God blazes at the world. Hell gapes for joy.
> And Europe whitens with those nameless tombs.
>
> Hesepe, 30 May

However, this 'weird backwater of the world' was where Bowman really came into his own: as Norman Kemp Smith put it, 'came to his full stature, as the man that imposed himself, as by natural right.'

Bowman himself said of this period in a letter to Mabel that he was 'working as never in my life before & with a perfect tremendous zest for all things of the mind.'

It was an extraordinary period of working under great pressure. He became the official translator for the camp, translating all official letters; he expanded his teaching into an educational programme and he wrote to the director of the RSA to have courses meet its syllabus requirements for certification; when a committee of prisoners was formed to run camp affairs, he was elected secretary; he became spokesman for the prisoners to the commandant; and he continued with what he saw as his creative achievement: writing his sonnets.

Day flowed into day with the intense work schedule Bowman gave himself and success fuelled his drive. He told Mabel: 'I feel that when I return I'll begin a new lease of mental life along with you. Never were the things of the mind nearer to me.' Chaplain Karney had also been transferred to Hesepe and his verdict on Bowman's philosophy lectures

> as well as their extraordinary success <u>as lectures</u>, shows me I have lost no power. He is a Cambridge honours man, accustomed to such things, & he told me that the lecture I gave last but one was the finest he had ever heard. And they're all almost impromptus. My own war experience has been a magnificent tonic & has braced & profited me beyond measure. And could I but be once more in touch with you my Dearest I feel I can stand anything until the day of release.

At the beginning of June, the censor stopped Bowman's first letter to Mabel:

> It won't be possible to tell you anything about the place or the situation here; & we must confine ourselves strictly to private affairs. Otherwise our letters will never get thro'. It's now over 2 months since I was taken, Darling, & I'm beginning to live in the near prospect of letters. To be in touch again! What a joy! And what an interval of waiting.

He told Mabel that he prayed for her each night and she was uppermost in his thoughts: 'Certain it is that you visit me constantly in dreams, & I think it is your own spirit seeking out mine across the spaces. I wish you could realize the intense spiritual energy & exaltation that constantly sustain me.'

In terms of his physical wellbeing, though, he did not get enough to sustain himself. The allied blockade of Germany was causing increasing hardship among the German people and there were consequences for the prisoners of war in their hands. The staple diet in the camps was soup, made from whatever the camp authorities could lay their hands on, so food parcels from home were vital in supplementing the prisoners' camp diet.

Throughout the summer, Bowman's letters and cards carried an urgent plea for food parcels. He told Mabel it was reported that Coopers the Grocers made up a good food parcel, 'but on no account are you to be extravagant, you will need everything for yourself & the children. Only what you can spare over for me.' He gave her some examples of what she might send: 'Tinned beans, sausages, mutton, sardines, bacon (all tinned); Horlicks, malted milk, tinned milk, tea, cheese, bully-beef.' He also asked her to send him some clothing, for he had had no change of clothes for two months. Yet he felt so bad about asking: 'forgive, forgive me!'

A captain who had just received a food parcel from home invited Bowman to join him for two evening meals. Bowman was gleeful: 'It was great! We had bully and biscuit, lard, cheese, & the second night a pudding he had made of rice & cocoa with lard.' Of course, one or two food parcels were inadequate for the whole camp. The Red Cross responded to the need and sent supplies until parcels arrived from home. 'I can hardly tell you what the bully-beef and the Swiss milk mean to me. I have such a craving for meat & for sweet stuff.' There were some Americans in the camp:

> The American parcels are simply lordly – tremendous affairs; but I should not care to be so lavishly supplied at a time like this; & <u>I do not want to exceed the home ration</u>. After all, the German soup kept us alive for 2½ to 3½ months; and it will count for something still.

Years later the Anglican chaplain Arthur Karney became Bishop of Johannesburg (he later became Bishop of Southampton), and he recalled the prison camp months and Bowman's contribution to camp life:

> He lectured on psychology without any books, on Shakespeare's tragedies… He gave a long course of philosophy, and took the higher German class – all without any books. We invited him into our mess because we felt that he was not looking after himself, but once he joined he insisted on sharing the cooking and washing-up.

The way Bowman saw it, he had been taken under the wing of a caring group of comrades:

> The kindness of my fellow-officers grows beyond all measure. A large number of them have begun to receive private parcels of food & these

they have shared freely with me. A party of RAMCs gave me a special dinner – perfectly wonderful – their own cooking & how proud they were to see me enjoy it. Tea is brought me every morning by the padre, one of the doctors or some other officer. I have been presented with English soap, shaving soap, a deck chair.

I have been taken possession of by a small group of splendid men, & compelled to take all my meals with them on condition that I accept all sorts of perquisites that are going & do nothing in the way of work. They cook for me, share their parcels with me, toast my bread for me & generally spoil me. You cannot imagine the overflowing goodness & kindness that besets me on every hand. The padre, Capt Karney, presides at our table (we call ourselves a syndicate). The other members are Capt Jones, a doctor; Lt Gates, a man of fine culture & a school-master; Lt Glenn, a very active business man.

By the end of June, Bowman was desperate for a letter from Mabel:

Would you have believed that it could ever become possible that we should not only be so long separated from each other but we should be without news of each other for weeks? An added sorrow is that the very strictly administered censorship forbids my telling you almost anything about my life here; so that you will have to wait – who knows how long? It may be years – until you hear it from my lips.

At last, on 11 July, almost three months to the day since he was captured, Bowman got not one letter but a bundle of letters from Mabel. Five days later, he wrote her a card:

Tonight my first parcel arrived. Probably it'll be a couple of days before I'm allowed to draw the contents. But it's such a joy to be in touch with you, in this way, Dearest & to feel your loving kindness about me. If clothes arrive they will be welcome. Imagine being between 3 & 4 months without coat, hat or a change & no means of procuring these.

The censor blacked out the remaining part. On the following Monday, Bowman received a parcel of clothes: 'My need was very great; & by a great stroke of fortune I had just been cleansed & was able to put on the pyjamas – as would otherwise have been impossible.'

That was the beginning of a steady flow of parcels: Mabel had rallied both their families and within weeks he had received five more food parcels. His physical wellbeing improved. 'My syndicate have toasted you again & again in bits of delicious cake etc. And yet I hate receiving anything in your own & my own country's need, & every parcel is a stab of kindness. And yet it is necessary, Dearest, & more so now than ever before.' In August he received three parcels, two from Mabel and one from his mother: 'They are the finest parcels I've had. The whole syndicate is so excited about them.'

When he insisted that he should take his turn at being chef, he had mixed results. 'On Sunday I was cook for the syndicate and it rather gave me a distaste for food. It was a big job & I did it unaided under very difficult conditions.' He outlined the menu for the day and told Mabel 'it was pronounced a perfect triumph; & very economical, as I worked in lots of scraps & leavings.' Well, at the time they may have been polite in declaring it a triumph; almost twenty years later, Bishop Karney could say: 'I'll never forget his first milk pudding.'

In these difficult conditions prisoners of war learned to improvise. Bowman described what they did with Berne biscuits: 'You bore a hole in them & pump water into them hard; then blow the water out with your mouth. Then you heat them; whereupon they swell & become like delicious new bread.' He also tried making pastry for a pie with a paste made out of biscuits rolled down with a lemonade bottle. 'You have no idea what a capable manager this life makes you. You'd laugh if I could enter into detail!'

He carried on writing his sonnets into July, but he wrote only seven under the *Hesepe* rubric; the last line of the seventh reads: 'Each morning Hesepe the lonely mocks!'

He then moved on to topics at a far remove from the war: subjects such as *Thoughts of Home*; another one *Watchwords and Maxims*. In the first of these he salutes Nietzsche for his aphorism: 'For, believe me, the secret of the greatest fruitfulness and the greatest enjoyment of existence is: to live dangerously!'

> 'Live Dangerously.' No braver mandate yet,
> Nietzsche, nor charged with finer lightning ran
> Around the world.

Then he concludes it with the sestet:

> One prayer I prayed: 'Lord, if Thou hast discerned
> Within me ought of manliness, enrol
> Thy servant with the fighters, who have earned
> Their manhood's charter where the thunders roll
> Over the field, that so I may have learned
> To taste this Element, and know my soul.'

The longest group he called *Influences*, and here he ranges widely in subjects from Homer to Russian literature and Wordsworth:

> Wordsworth, above all poets in thee I find
> What in the greatest we too seldom see,
> The crowning virtue of tranquillity,
> Effectual o'er the sorrows of the mind.

He writes of his early devotion to philosophy:

> Underneath the blows
> Of thought I laboured long in labouring seas,
> Pledging my soul to martyred Socrates;
> And o'er night's face the star of Plato rose.

The last two poems he dated 25 July. One of the two has the theme of religious faith and ends with the line: 'Earth's glory sinks confronted with Christ's cross.'

He had compiled a volume that he thought might be published. However, he had a problem: thirty-six of his most vivid and emotionally-charged verses were being held at Rastatt prison camp. There was nothing he could do about it on his own, but at Hesepe he gained a patron.

In Jean Renoir's classic film of 1937, *La Grande Illusion*, the setting is largely in a German prisoner-of-war camp (Renoir himself had been a PoW), and one of the key themes that affects the outcome is the chivalrous mutual regard of the commandant (played by Erich von Stroheim) and a French prisoner (Pierre Fresnay); both men were aristocrats and both had been aviators.

A similar sort of scenario developed in Hesepe between the commandant and Bowman. Both were academics and each had a respect for the other's country and culture. As a result: 'The Commandant has been very kind & has exerted himself to recover my poems from Rastatt, & these are now promised in due course. This will enable me to complete my volume… I am deeply grateful to the German commandant for his efforts & for his sympathy.'

In due course the sonnets arrived from Rastatt and when Bowman felt he now had a collection that could form a book, he wrote a Foreword to it:

> For allowing this slight volume to see the light of day I have but one excuse to offer. The situation to which these verses are the emotional reaction represents a very real and serious piece of experience. It is no mere poetical exaggeration to say that in the first days of captivity at least, the writing of the sonnets was a labour that 'stood between my soul and madness', and

> I cannot help feeling that what, under one of the heaviest blows that can befall a soldier, has meant so much to me, may have in it something that will raise it at times above the personal to the level of general human interest.

Anticipating criticism for defects in his rhyme scheme in places, he drafted an apologia:

> The irregularity of the rime form in some of the opening sonnets I cannot justify except on the grounds of a certain breathlessness in the theme and in the execution. Later I had thoughts of amending this fault; but I felt that whatever might be the poetical quality of the pieces affected, no real improvement was likely to result from any such merely technical revision; and I resolved to leave what I had written at a heat, in the certainty that the rime order in the sestet was not the factor by which the merit of individual sonnets or of the volume as a whole would be judged.

At his final revision, however, he had a change of heart and scored it out. Then he concluded the Foreword with a noble gesture:

> It ought to be a pleasure to acknowledge generosity in an enemy; and I wish to express my indebtedness to Captain Hohnholz, Commandant of the Prison-Camp at Hesepe, to whose kindness I owe it that I am able to offer the sonnets as they stand for publication.
> *Offizier-Gefangenenlager*
>
> Hesepe, 17th August 1918

***

Back home in Britain, that summer of 1918 marked four years of living with the shadow of death cast over the land.

Mabel and Jennie Mackay took a house in Eli, on the Firth of Forth, for the month of July. Jennie's baby was due in August. She had gone through a worrying time when her husband was involved in both the spring offensives. Now there was a respite. Harry's battalion, the 14th HLI, was reduced to a cadre that would be absorbed into other battalions and Harry was awaiting orders to be reassigned.

It was six months since Bowman had left home. His children missed their father and he was missing out on key stages of their development. With her teacher-training background, Mabel was aware of this and flagged up scenes from their young lives so that Archie would have a record of them. Ian and Maisie loved that month on the coast, playing in the sand and paddling in the sea. For a time, Maisie copied everything Ian did and said. Then she went through a feisty independent stage; when she was displeased with her mother she would say to her: 'Go away Mammy, go away Germany.' Ian was the leader, though, and conscious of it when it came to decisions. There was the option to vary their wartime diet and Mabel told the children they were going to have rabbit for their meal. Ian protested: 'But we don't want to eat rabbits, we want to keep them.'

The timing of the holiday let for the month of July was finely judged: Jennie's baby daughter was born on 8 August. Mabel told Archie, 'she is a real little beauty girl. I am much charmed by her and just wish we were having another little chick-a-biddy.'

When Mabel had written to Harry Mackay in April to see if he knew what had happened to Archie, she mentioned in passing that Harry was a very lucky man to be married to Jennie. In his reply to Mabel, telling her what he had heard about Archie, Harry returned to her comments about his luck in having Jennie:

> I have been most interested in Ian's birthday party. Jennie wrote about it and described it. She enjoyed herself hugely. I'm so glad you think she is looking so well, and I <u>do</u> know how much you love her, and how very much she loves you too.
>
> But why, Mabel, do you say that I'm in the fortunate position of <u>just beginning</u> to know my luck? Oh Mabel, my dear, I knew and loved Jennie long, long ago, and there was a terrible lot more than luck in the happy circumstances that brought us together again. But I never really realised before (in the old days I mean) just the full significance of having Jennie as my own. I do now though, Mabel, and I have felt so wonderfully happy <u>ever since the very first night you asked me along at Leven</u>. I wish I could get home to see Jennie and you all at home. Just a terrible longing possesses me, Mabel. But I feel altogether different this time in France. Last time I didn't care if I never went home, and I <u>didn't</u> go home when I got the chance. But <u>now</u> there is Jennie, and it's all the difference.

Some men had no close bonding, no life partner or special friend to come home to. Such a one was the third of the trio of British academics at Princeton University serving their country (according to the *New York Times* article): George Glover. A modern linguist and a graduate of Manchester University, he had been a lecturer at Marburg University in Germany before going to Princeton. He was in the 1st Battalion, Rifle Brigade. He and Bowman kept in touch, but in 1916 Bowman had been remiss in writing. Glover, who had been in France for two weeks, began one of his letters: 'My Dear Bowman, Are you aware it is four months since a word or sign has come from you? And apparently you have treated friends in Princeton no better, to judge from Hendel's most recent letter.' He finished off with: 'Give my kindest regards to Mrs Bowman and also to Ian. I want a report of his progress as he is one of the very few babies I know.'

Later, for his part in an action in the line, Lieutenant Glover was awarded the DSO. When he heard that Bowman had been captured, he wrote to Mabel to pass on information:

> Tell Mr Bowman his condolences were a trifle previous – I've made a DSO out of it. I can't believe it myself yet, it still takes my breath away and without any false modesty I do most honestly feel that what little I did was less my own doing than merely being there while the men – always the real heroes – did it. However, the officers catch the limelight, and I shan't refuse it. But it will be a strain to live up to it.

Modest George Glover was not given long to live up to it. On 1 September 1918 he died of wounds received in August. On 8 September, when Mabel learned of it she wrote to Archie: 'Oh my Dear, Glover died of wounds, and I've just heard that.' The shock at the news affected her: 'I'm very sad. I'll follow instructions about writing.' Glover's death stayed with her. A week later she wrote:

> Dearest, all day I have been so sad and depressed about Mr Glover. I am feeling his loss very deeply though altogether it wasn't for a very long time that we knew him. Still he is associated with that beautiful wonderful time when our little Eenie was coming and had come and the thought that he will never again sit in our porch makes me very sad. I think dear I was really fonder of him than you were. I think he had a very beautiful refined soul Archie. Oh dear it is all so very sad. He was 33 but he was just beginning to live I think when he came to America. He expected to be on leave soon and I was hoping to be able to ask him here for a few days. He has no very close friends I think to mourn his loss yet somehow to my mind that makes it all the sadder for in a few years he would likely have been coming into his own.

All the while that a generation of men was being cast into oblivion, women shouldered the burden of family responsibilities and commitments. Mabel rose to the task. She took action on the lease of their house in Princeton and told Archie: 'I felt that with you a prisoner we simply must give it up when our lease was out.' Having taken action, she also had to learn to live with frustration when she was told that they could not get off the hook as terminating the lease involved the agreement of two other parties.

She also took the initiative and found out about her entitlement to children's allowances – the area that so concerned Archie – and she intended to withdraw money from the bank on the blank cheques she had. 'Don't worry about me dear. I can easily raise the wind. There are heaps of people who would very gladly lend me money to tide over this time. I'd probably ask Norrie K. [Norman Kemp Smith] as I feel he is closer to you than anyone in spirit.'

Still, the separation was hard for Mabel: 'I'm so weary for word of you again dear heart and longing to know that all is well with you.' She remembered difficult times in the past for them:

> Do you remember the other parting before you went to Leipzig? Would you believe it dear that we came nearest to breaking my heart but you see I've survived it and as have you. We'll survive this too dearest, God willing and what right glad people we'll all be 'when Archie comes marching home.' I sent off a parcel of books to you yesterday from Smiths. Shakespeare, Chaucer, *The Scarlet Letter* and *Sense and Sensibility*.

Occasionally, she allowed herself to daydream. When Thomas Beecham was conducting opera in Glasgow, she wrote: 'If you were here dearest and we could leave the children I'd be wanting to go very often.' Even when she was low herself, Mabel tried to cheer her husband. A prisoner of war who had been repatriated wrote to Mabel. She told Archie that the letter came from 'a Capt Rogers who is back in London from Hesepe. It's quite a short note but very appreciative of your work in camp. Dear, dear Archie I know just how you would be.'

However, life with the Stewart family was becoming more trying. Her father had become very deaf and insisted on hearing everything that was said 'unless he's asleep. There's going to be a great deal of strain this coming winter.'

Then things got even worse. Theresa, the servant employed by the Stewarts for a few years, left at short notice. However much Mabel had reservations about her standards, she still did the work and finding a replacement by the autumn of 1918 was no easy task. Mabel found that servants were 'about impossible to get.' So she had to take on yet another role in a house with coal fires and few labour-saving conveniences and was 'hard at it keeping this unwieldy house in order.' Her mother was no longer up to the task of running the home, her energy

> expended in dancing attendance on Father. O Archie my own, how thankful I am that yours is an altogether different conception of manhood from what I was brought up to respect. I think Johnnie and I are the only two in the family who have revoked it altogether. It seems strange that we

should be the two who have been fated to live longest under the same roof and in constant touch with the old thing.

While Johnnie, as Mabel said, had been fated to live longest under the Stewart family roof, he had gone his own way: he had a job as a measurer and he developed his own interests. He wrote to his brother-in-law in prison camp in cheery terms and asked him about opportunities for studying:

> Have you any chance of learning Russian? Mine is discontinued for the present, but I mean to keep at it on and off. I got a Russian gospel of St Mark in Manchester for 1 penny so I have a text I can easily carry about with me for the odd moment.

Mabel was by now overworked by coping with her new range of domestic duties and it was unfair on Ian and Maisie, she felt, because she could not give them as much time as she should. She got a teenage girl to come in and spend time with them. Also, as well as keeping the small family together and running the Stewart household, Mabel, in a sense, had to feed and clothe a third child: she was responsible for ensuring her husband's wellbeing in the prison camp. Bowman acknowledged it: 'I am sad to think that I need to be fed like a child & am so useless to all my dearest.' She organized food parcels for him from herself and the wider family, and she planned to provide him with warm clothing. As early as the month of August, she was thinking ahead: 'How will winter be in the camp with winds sweeping across those melancholy plains?'

***

As early as September, it was obvious to the prisoners that winter in the makeshift camp at Hesepe would be grim. A camp committee was reconvened: Major Faber was chairman and Bowman was voted secretary for the second time. He was also far from idle while the *Kommandantur*, the German high command, came to a decision on whether his collection of sonnets could be sent to the enemy country for publication:

> Dearest, I am almost overwhelmed with work & in our little prison community I am of use. For the second time I've been elected (three weeks ago) to a small committee that runs the business of the camp – huge majorities in my favour each time; so you see even as a business man I am in demand here. I have also regular courses in logic, psychology, advanced German, & (at present) on *Hamlet*. <u>I translate all official</u> letters,

> & in addition I study every available moment. Oh how I wish you could have my poems! I don't know yet whether I'll be able to publish them. The Commandant saw me today about it, & told me it would take a long time to give a decision. Of course they'll all have to be examined. If I am not allowed to send them home for publication, I've asked to be allowed to lodge one copy with Prof. Riehl [Professor Alois Riehl of Berlin University under whom Bowman had studied] & one with the Dutch Ambassador to keep for me till the war is over.

Some books had reached him from his family, and on 5 September Norman Kemp Smith wrote to him enclosing

> a Wordsworth and some 8 volumes from the 'Everyman' library. Trust the Dante has meantime reached you. Shall be glad if you can indicate for me in letters to your wife any books that you and your companions in captivity would specially like to have. I shall be only too delighted to have the privilege of sending them.

Earlier he had suggested to Bowman: 'How about translating Kant's *Kritik der reinen Vernunft* [*Critique of Pure Reason*] and other ethical writings? That is a worth-while enterprise, badly needed in view of the unsatisfactoriness of Abbott's translation, and it is work that the camp authorities are likely to be willing to give you facilities for.' However, Bowman had already written a letter a month earlier (which Kemp Smith would have not yet received): 'Any work involving concentrated mental effort is very hard in an emergency camp.'

By this stage at Hesepe prison camp, there was what Bowman called 'a tremendous educational programme' in place: 'it included Latin, Greek, French, German (I take the advanced class in this), Mathematics, Philosophy, Psychology, Music, Tamil, Shorthand, Italian, Portuguese, Art, Hindustani (Urdu), First Aid & a Bible Class. Of course I take the Philosophy & Psychology.'

Since some of the prisoners who were teaching these subjects were qualified teachers, the idea came up that they could follow syllabuses of the Royal Society of Arts and in due course ex-PoWs might gain accreditation or sit exams in the UK.

Bowman drafted a letter to Sir Alfred T. Davies, KBE, CB at the Victoria & Albert Museum in South Kensington, who was chairman and director of the 'British Prisoners of War Book Scheme'; he explained that there were certain classes taught by 'qualified teachers' and 'it is proposed that these classes be adapted to the RSA requirements', and asked if syllabuses could be supplied for different levels.

The British Prisoners of War Book Scheme was a greatly appreciated service in the prison camps. In April 1918, the editor of *The Spectator* magazine had published a letter from Sir Alfred making an appeal for books for the scheme. Sir Alfred wrote that repatriated prisoners had delivered messages to him from 'the heads of several of the educational organizations in internment camps in enemy countries served by our Book Scheme.' He appealed for a wide range of books. 'If it were realized that there are probably more earnest (male) students in these internment camps than in all the universities in the British Empire put together… there would, I am sure, be an overwhelming response to my appeal.'

Nevertheless, while the educational programme could help keep up the prisoners' morale, the prospect of winter loomed near and the camp committee, at their meeting of 7 September, instructed their spokesman, Bowman, 'to make the most forcible representations' to the German general who was due to visit the camp on the following points:

1. That this camp is not, and cannot be considered a camp fit for officers, that this fact has been repeatedly acknowledged by the German authorities, and yet that no steps are being taken to remove officers to a suitable camp or camps, although immediate action was promised on this several weeks ago.
2. That in the event of no redress being found possible, and officers being faced with the possibility of having to spend the winter or part of the winter in Hesepe, the following indispensable improvements be introduced without delay.

Their requests included the provision of hot baths once a week; a drying room; the issue of peat should be supplemented with an issue of wood to enable cooks to kindle fires in the morning; a windbreak screen to be erected at the door of the cookhouse; the sleeping hut to be subdivided; and 'that a party of four officers be allowed to visit Osnabrück once a week.'

This last request was far from ludicrous. An agreement had been reached between the German and British governments as early as 1916 that officers should be allowed to walk outside the camp in small groups, providing they gave their parole that they would not try to escape. The camp authorities could readily make this concession and Bowman's parole pass was a small orange card dated 20 August 1918, printed in German and English:

> I, herewith, give my word of honour that I shall not, in case of my taking part in a walk, make an attempt to escape during such walk, i.e. from the time of leaving the camp until having returned to it, and not to commit

any acts that are directed against the safety of the German Empire. I know that, according to 159 of the M.-St.-G.-B. [*sic*, definition unknown] a prisoner of war, who escapes in despite of the word of honour given, is liable to death.

I also give my word of honour to use this card only myself and not to give it to any other prisoner of war.

Bowman got his first walk outside the camp in late September: 'Oh how wonderful to be out of the cage & strolling along a country road in exquisite autumn afternoon!'

Having given his word of honour, there was no thought of trying to escape when he was out on parole, but he did think of escaping from inside the camp and there were different possibilities. One option meant enlisting the help of a guard and he rejected this on moral grounds. According to his brother Alex:

A story slipped out one night, after his captivity in Germany, when we were talking about some of his experiences and his thoughts about the possibility of escape from the prison camp: 'To have done so,' he said, 'would really have been quite simple', for one of the guards had established such friendly and sympathetic relations with him that little more than a simple request would have opened the door to him. But, he said, 'I couldn't do it… I couldn't ask a fellow man to fall into the guilt of treachery.'

Bowman had another method in mind, if he could have back-up papers and German marks, and he saw a way of getting them when Captain Karney was told he was being repatriated early. Karney would be in London, and Bowman asked him to take a message to Norman Kemp Smith at the Ministry of Information. The message from Bowman was later related by Kemp Smith:

I was to find a way of sending him, in the binding of the books that I was regularly forwarding to him, a German map, and if possible some German money and identity papers. I had no hesitation in at once saying that Bowman's life was much too precious to be risked in any desperate venture, and I would do nothing of the kind.

Karney agreed with Kemp Smith, but had fulfilled his promise to Bowman to bring the message.

However, the strain of separation from Mabel was beginning to tell on Bowman: 'Darling, it is utterly useless trying to write you as my heart would, under the circumstances. You will have to feel it all – unspoken.' As he felt Mabel's loneliness come through in her letters, the restrictions he was under made it all the more frustrating. He replied in response to one of Mabel's letters: 'Dearest, I know how lonely and desolate you feel, and I would love to write fully and freely to you. These cards & letter-cards almost chill me whenever I try to write to you on them. It's impossible to write as I would like.' Another reply reads:

> More than ever I simply live in the thought of you & for that future. Sometimes the vividness of my consciousness is almost unendurable. My poems are finished... I have worked at tremendous pressure, & have a sense of having carried thro' my greatest achievement. Now I have a philosophy lecture followed by a psychology one.

Archie longed to see his children. He tried to imagine the way they had developed in the months since he had seen them, and he wrote a special card to Ian:

> This is just a wee post-card to tell you that Daddy is thinking about you and loving you every day, as he is doing to our dearest Mammy and our own wee Girlie Gee. I think you must be a right, big strong boy now, and you must be very kind and loving to our Mammy and be a good boy to her as you promised your Daddy the day he went off to the war. Daddy cannot get home to you, but he will get home some day & we will all be very glad.

In Hesepe the camp committee met frequently throughout September. Not all its business addressed issues with the German authorities; a lieutenant in the Northumberland Fusiliers had a bee in his bonnet about keeping up standards among the prisoners and submitted an item for consideration: 'To maintain dignity of British officers in general by punishing in some way all officers who persist in arriving late on roll-call parades and who appear in semi-dressed condition and whose general appearance is certain to lower our prestige.' Bowman did not minute the outcome.

What was important to the prisoners was whether or not their submission to the general would result in improvements to their living conditions at Hesepe. At the end of September, the German high command responded: the prisoners were to be moved. So the priority for the camp committee when it met on 30 September was the impending move to Cologne and on 10 October they were moved to a camp there.

Now settled into more substantial quarters, Bowman found the rest of October passed quickly. On 6 November he wrote a card to his little girl Maisie who was soon to be 2 years old: 'This is a wee post-card to let you know that Daddy is looking forward to your birthday & that he wishes you many happy returns, & will be thinking of you all the time when you are having your birthday party. This is a birthday kiss for you X.'

Just five days later, the war was over.

Köln, 11th November 1918

My Very Own Most Precious Mabel,
Whether this will ever reach you I know not; but it is to assure you that everything is absolutely and utterly well with me. There is not the slightest need for anxiety. I am absolutely safe, well & happy. No letters have reached me for a long time & no parcels have come for ever so long; but we live in daily hope; & in these great times we can well afford to be patient. Can you realize it Beloved? In a few short weeks I may well be stepping into No. 77 Montgomerie Street. Why I may be home for your dear, dear Birthday, if not for our Maisie-Mes. But if not, Beloved, this will convey my dearest love & my fond, fond wishes for many happy returns – returns on which I shall be with you to show you my love & fondness in a better way than this. How I should love to write you the history of these days; but it is better to wait; & what a long wonderful story I'll have to tell. You'll have all my poems to read. Today they were returned to me from the *Kommandantur*.

We are all agog with the utmost excitement & the highest expectations; & visions of home-coming float daily before my eyes. – What a time it will be. How many, many a night I have lain awake in bed & far into the small hours of the morning picturing it all. And now it seems to be an approaching reality. My deepest love meanwhile to all at home – to my Eenie & Maisie, to Mother and your Mother & Alick & Johnnie & the Aunt. My best wishes to your Grandpa. I will make this short, so that it'll have a better chance of getting through. And so, till we meet, infinite joy & tender love to my Mabel! How good God has been to bring us thro' so much in safety. How little we have been called upon to sacrifice compared to others. How great the joy after your agony of sorrow & suspense. For ever

Your Archie X

That morning of 11 November, however, when the slaughter was to cease at 11.00 am and the bells would ring out across the country, there was a cruel irony to the telegram that was delivered to 77 Montgomerie Street for Mabel.

It contained six words that chilled her: 'Jennie passed away this morning. Suddenly. Cathie.'

***

Ten days after the signing of the Armistice, Bowman left the prisoner-of-war camp. He knew Cologne from trips there when he was a student. The steamer *Rex Rheni* had been commandeered to sail down the Rhine to Rotterdam and he got a place on it. The ship cast off on 21 November. Bowman disembarked at Nijmegen on the first stage of the journey back to Blighty. The precise stages of the following movements are not known but he seems to have reported to Ripon, where he was given two months' leave. Then he must have sent a telegram, for Mabel was expecting him. She arranged things the way she wanted them, but she did not tell the children; it was to be the supreme surprise for them.

It was 30 November, St Andrew's Day. Many years later Ian wrote about his father's homecoming and Ian took it from the viewpoint of the children that day, but he wrote it in the third person:

> The children were playing in the dining room, while Mabel moved restlessly about the house, trying to occupy herself with minor domestic tasks. As she looked into the dining room to see how the children were behaving, the doorbell rang. The children heard her give a little cry, and she ran to the door. Intuitively the children felt that something unusual was happening, and after a moment, when their mother did not return, they crept into the hall. They saw their mother being held firmly by a strange-looking man. She was crying. This was too much for Ian who ran at the man and started to hit him. The man picked him up and hugged him laughing, and carried him into the dining room, where Maisie had retreated for safety under the table. Mabel brought her out and said, 'This is your daddy-man, home from the war.' As comprehension dawned, the children made a wild rush at him. He picked them both up and marched round the room triumphantly, with Mabel laughing at his side. Archie Bowman's war was over.

Chapter Five

Gatekeeper

I am not cut out for the role of conquering hero, and to place my foot on the necks of fallen enemies is quite alien to my temperament.

Archie Bowman

Barely three months after having to sleep on a mattress stuffed with packing paper in a prison camp, Lieutenant Archie Bowman was back in Cologne and had a posh billet in a mansion on Spichernstrasse: 'I never slept in such a bed. The linen was so fine it felt like silk, and the rich warm coverlets were so fine that they felt like a featherweight.' There was also night-life: one evening he had had a seat in the box of the Opera House for a production of Wagner's *Der fliegende Holländer* [*The Flying Dutchman*]. Two boxes along to his left sat General Plumer, the commander of the British Army of the Rhine, with a bevy of staff officers.

The seat Bowman had was right in the centre, facing the stage; the boxes ran the whole way round. The performance was 'absolutely superb – the singing simply overwhelming.' He was moved by the haunting melodies and the excellent stagecraft: the lighting and the sound; the spirit-movement on the phantom ship; the dark mysterious crew that rose like ghosts on the captain's whistle; and the unrolling of the morning mists to show sunlit seas.

His immediate boss in his new job, Captain Prior, had taken a box. There was a seat available, Prior offered it to him and Bowman paid him for it. During the intervals the two men strolled about in the vast corridors. Bowman found it strange: there were two distinct audiences – Germans, predominantly women, and British officers – keeping entirely to themselves. The British officers stood aloof, in groups, 'watching the General perambulate.'

The cultural life was rich in Cologne and theatre-going was not expensive: a box seat cost 8 marks [about 4 shillings]. Prior urged Bowman that he should go to the opera at least once a week. The programme for the spring season included *Tannhäuser*, *Fidelio*, *Figaro* and *Madam Butterfly*.

At long last the man who in the space of a year played many parts – combat soldier, PoW, sonneteer, translator, teacher and spokesman for his comrades – walked through the doorway of 77 Montgomerie Street, Glasgow as he had done many times in his dreams, was reunited with Mabel and the children and became a family man again. However, he was a returned prisoner of war on leave, the army had not released him and he had orders to return to his battalion at Haddington, East Lothian at the end of January.

After he was settled into the Stewart home, on 5 December Bowman wrote to his old mentor, colleague and friend:

> My Dear Kemp Smith,
>
> It seems almost an impertinence to try and thank you in words for all you have done for me and mine in the long months of my captivity. Of course I depended on you implicitly and I knew that you would act just as you did. It is none the less a true delight to read your letters and telegrams – those especially bearing on those first trying weeks – and to hear from my wife and mother of all your kindness and invaluable practical aid. The consciousness that it would be forthcoming did much to render my own troubles endurable. Although I cannot thank you in words, I will try harder than ever in some measure to prove worthy of the friendship which I will always place first in my life. With your own goodness to me and mine I identify that of Mrs Kemp Smith, whose ministrations did much to cheer and succour us; and it will always be a pleasure to think that it was one of her Edinburgh parcels that enabled a little group of us to stave off the pangs of hunger on our lingering journey down the Rhine.

Bowman also thanked him for his patience in meeting Captain Karney and a fellow repatriated prisoner, his 'emissaries of conspiracy', and listening to his escape plan, which Kemp Smith had deliberately not followed up.

However, it was now the future that they both had to look to, and their civilian jobs. Kemp Smith had briefed Bowman that Warren Fite, chair of the Philosophy Department at Princeton, had written to say they did not have to return to Princeton until the autumn. That was a relief to Bowman for, at this stage, he did not know what the War Office had in mind for him next.

The Great War was over, but the tectonic plates of the political crust had been in motion in Russia, Germany and Britain.

The Russian Revolution brought the Bolshevik government to power and it struck a separate peace with Germany; the Czech legions that fought in Russia on the allied side were trapped. The allies sent an expeditionary force to help extricate them, although the allies also had their own strategic objectives for doing this.

In Germany, in the last month of the war sailors mutinied, soldiers' councils sprang up, and in Berlin in January a radical group of communists led by Rosa Luxemburg and Karl Liebknecht sparked off the Spartacist armed uprising.

In Britain there was insurrection: first the unfurling of the banner in Dublin 'We serve neither King nor Kaiser, but Ireland'; in 1916 there had been the armed Easter Rising; and in the General Election of 1918 Sinn Féin swept the board in Ireland, refused to send its elected members to the Westminster parliament, formed an Irish assembly in Dublin and drew up a draft constitution for a Republic of Ireland.

Along Clydeside, tremors were being felt in the Glasgow that Bowman left in January to return to his unit and, on 31 January, they erupted into strikes, massed meetings and the George Square riots. The police lost control. The government, anxious lest the Spartacist uprising in Berlin could be replicated in the UK, sent in tanks and troops. However, the troops in Maryhill Barracks, depot of the HLI (the City of Glasgow Regiment) were not deployed in case they sympathized with the strikers.

However, seismic waves travelled as far as Haddington where two companies of Bowman's HLI battalion 'had a demonstration that amounted almost to mutiny': they were refusing to parade for physical training and bayonet-fighting. It was an indication of unrest and strikes in the country and senior officers played it down. Bowman told Mabel that a general was sent for

> and remonstrated with them, but up to now they have not gone back to that part of their work. A few months ago such a state of affairs would have been almost unthinkable. It is of course symptomatic of the general unrest. I read with anxiety about the situation in Glasgow; and I sincerely trust, Beloved, that things won't go much further.

Reflecting to Kemp Smith on recent developments, Bowman looked at the situation in Ireland: 'it seems to me that in the light of the election returns, we can no longer withhold her independence from Ireland – should she express an unambiguous desire for it.' He did not question Britain's role in intervening militarily in Russia; he told Kemp Smith: 'If there were any chance of limited service there, Russia is the place where I should like to go; but it looks as if the forces of occupation there were to be on the old-time regular basis, with extended engagement, which of course would not suit me at all.'

On the wider plain, Bowman felt concerned about the haste with which America was demobilizing: 'In view of the general situation I think she might have postponed that operation.'

At this stage in his thinking, he had not studied the idea of a League of Nations as the way forward to ensure world peace. He focused on the post-Armistice negotiations:

> It is a trying thing to be kept so much in the dark as to the proceedings of the Peace Conference. I am not over-enthusiastic as to the League of

> Nations, tho' I think some such scheme promises to smooth over some outstanding difficulties in the present negotiations. It is a good thing too to strike out on fresh lines under influence of ideas. What I am a little afraid of is that the final issue will not be a league of nations but two or more hostile or latently hostile groups.

However, as yet his mind was still reliving war experiences and his reaction to what he had been through, and he confessed to Kemp Smith: 'I find it difficult to accommodate myself to the new world which has sprung into being over-night. The removal of the familiar shadow in which we have been living so long requires a level of mental readjustment which can hardly be easy or painless.' He was expressing a fellow feeling for Kemp Smith, who had confided to him that he had gone through a period of malaise and depression when the war ended and his work at the Ministry of Information became redundant. In encouraging his Princeton colleague, Bowman wrote: 'Your achievement has been a wonderful one – the building up and pushing through of all that propaganda work, and on top of that the completion of your magnum opus.'

When Bowman had been on leave he met William Macneile Dixon, who had been home on Christmas leave in Glasgow. Dixon, head of the propaganda section in the Ministry of Information that dealt with influencing American public opinion, had been full of praise for Kemp Smith's work. Soon Dixon would be returning to Glasgow University where he held the chair in English Language and Literature, and he told Bowman that he was very keen to see Kemp Smith back in a university in Scotland, preferably Glasgow. He sounded out Bowman in case there was anything in Kemp Smith's attitude that might prove an obstacle. Bowman reassured him on that score, and he passed this all on to Kemp Smith.

Then the gateway into Bowman's own short-term future in the army opened in February when Secretary of State for War Winston Churchill confirmed to the House of Commons that the government would retain both fighting soldiers and repatriated prisoners of war during the period of the Armies of Occupation. So Bowman was sent back to Germany, to Cologne. His first job was at a school, teaching subjects for university to officers, men whose studies had been interrupted by war service.

The training school was based in the *Handelsschule* and a nearby restaurant was the mess. Bowman was billeted in a mansion on Spichernstrasse. When he arrived, the door was opened by a smart maid and he found himself in an elegant house with marble stairs. The family appeared: they consisted of an elderly Herr Heusmann, his daughter and his son. They treated him with impeccable courtesy and respect: 'I was quite embarrassed. I'm afraid I'm not cut out for the role of conquering hero, and to place my foot on the necks of fallen enemies is quite alien to my temperament.' The family conducted him to his room, which had been the son's room, and some of his clothes were still there. Bowman winced and expressed his regret that he was compelled to put them to this trouble. Herr Heusmann replied that it was the war.

Scarcely any of the British officers Bowman came across had ever set foot in Germany before. To them, the Germans had been 'the Hun', 'Jerry', 'Fritz' the enemy, and some officers had been primed with stories of German atrocities. Bowman observed how they responded to being in contact with German civilians:

> I think there is a certain danger of officers falling in love with Germany. The extraordinary courtesy of the people has shaken them visibly, and I can see two distinct types of reaction. There are those that are visibly impressed and shaken, and there are those who, while admitting the facts, seek to harden their hearts by cursing and damning the Bosch for 'being so damned polite'.

His superior billet was lit by electricity and Bowman was impressed by the two-way switches 'which are ingeniously arranged so that you can give yourself light on coming in late at night, and extinguish the light behind you as you go up to your bedroom, without returning on your tracks.'

When he arrived at the billet on the second evening, Bowman found the family in the dining room, awaiting his arrival. Herr Heusmann came out into the hall at once and invited Bowman to join them. The family was sharing a bottle of wine. Bowman was offered a glass, but explained that he was teetotal. Immediately a maid was sent to bring a bottle of soda water for him. Next Herr Heusmann offered him a cigar but Bowman opted for a cigarette instead. They gathered round the table, and

> then Herr Heusmann proceeded to open formal negotiations with the enemy. He began by proposing that the war should be banned as a subject of conversation – to which I readily assented. He told me it was a good thing I spoke German as he had not a single word of English. We arranged all little matters having to do with our mutual relations, and I was repeatedly enjoined to lay all my *Wünsche* [requests] before them, and these would at once be complied with. As regards service, I was told about the personal characteristics of the two maids, and I was asked whether I wished my bedroom done by the maid or by my batman. I referred the question to Miss Heusmann, who preferred that the maid do the room.

One evening at the theatre Bowman heard a song that struck a poignant memory for him, and he told Mabel about it:

> Do you remember how you loved that song? You wrote to me about it in Germany long, long ago. It was one of Jennie's songs, and we heard it together at that concert so long ago at Eastpark Church, just shortly after I got to know Jennie. Hearing it here touched me deeply and made me feel how art lifts us out of time and place into an eternal sphere of its own.

Just a week or so later there was another reminder of the sudden loss of Jennie when a fellow officer told Bowman that he had seen Harry Mackay in Cologne. 'How I should like to meet him,' Bowman wrote to Mabel, 'I think I'll drop a note to his unit, wherever it is, and let him know where I am, and maybe we can arrange a meeting.'

Teaching at the *Handelsschule*, however, turned out to be short-lived: Bowman was transferred to the Civil Permit Office of the British Army of the Rhine, which was also in Cologne, where there was urgent need of a German-speaking British army officer.

Under the powers assumed by the occupying forces after the Armistice, the occupied territory was divided among the British, Americans, French and Belgian authorities. German civilians had to have a permit in order to travel from the area under British control into that of any other area or into the unoccupied area or travel to another country. Those wishing to travel had to appear in front of a British officer, and they had to hand over an elaborate form with all their details and the reason for travelling.

On 17 February Bowman had his first day on the job. He had to 're-examine the circumstances of the case and decide whether such a pass can be given.' In his first day he managed to deal with 200 applicants, but he reckoned he could speed that up. It was good practice for him reading German Gothic script and in getting the hang of local speech idioms. All sorts of people wanted to travel. In a letter to Kemp Smith, Bowman gave examples of the kind of characters travelling that, years later, could have been in the script of a Federico Fellini film:

> The applications come from every grade of society – commercial travellers, actors and actresses, members of the national assembly, strolling show people, lion-tamers, itinerant preachers and people of obscure religious sects, people who have access to a supply of potatoes somewhere, numbers of invalids seeking a cure, suspects trying to break through (we keep a black-list and are always ready to arrest members of it). It is interesting to note the number of people certified to be suffering

from nervous breakdown and ordered away for a cure, the number of children who have broken down from undernourishment and are ordered by the doctor to be removed to another part of the country where food is more plentiful.

As he got into the swing of the work, he was surprised to find that it was more interesting than he had expected:

> I am beginning to have more to do with the people themselves, and this is what I want. A constant stream of all nationalities passes through our office, with all sorts of difficulties and complications. In fact it is about the best work I've had to do in the army, and I should be reluctant to go back to educational work, where I should be dealing entirely with our own men.

One of the things Bowman soon learned was how to seize the gist of a request and make a quick decision, but he also had to keep a lookout for 'suspects', as he termed them, for intelligence had furnished the Permit Office with a blacklist.

One day a real oddball of an old man turned up in the office. He had 'a most appalling wheeze', but what first registered with Bowman was his accent. Captain Cohen was the officer dealing with the man's application and Bowman was aware that Cohen had a lot to say and a lot to listen to. Eventually, they gave the old fellow a seat on the sidelines and sent a German clerk to bring him a glass of water. Then another officer came across to Bowman and whispered to him that the applicant was one of his countrymen. Bowman took that as a hint and went across to interview him. He looked a wreck, he had a tremor and seemed miserable. He was a Scotsman, and he said he came from Honnef. His story was that he had been in Germany when war broke out and had to stay. His hometown in Scotland, he said, was 'Cumbernau'd' [Cumbernauld]; he pronounced it with the omission of the 'l' as in spoken Scots. After the strange applicant had gone, Captain Cohen and a colleague came over to Bowman to query him about the man's accent: they suspected that he was a German spy. All Bowman could confirm was that whatever he may have been, he was certainly a Scotsman.

The work interested Bowman; he had no hankering to return to teaching now that he was in contact with German people, and he was getting insight into what was happening to them after the war. He told Kemp Smith about the plight of demobilized German soldiers whose civilian clothes had been left in another city or part of the country and who were not allowed to travel to collect them; until a few days earlier, they were not even allowed to have them sent by post:

They cannot re-equip themselves owing to the exorbitant prices. The result is large numbers have to wear out their uniforms – removing the buttons and other distinctively military emblems. Since leaving Cologne in November, I see a very marked decline in the conditions of life. I think the people are very near the line of starvation now. We used to be able to get pastry in the shops. Now the food shops are almost empty, and pastry is a dream of the past. The weekly meat ration would hardly make one fair meal. Morale is very low. The children are getting wild. The streets are not kept so clean as of old. Everywhere there is an air of decay and deep depression.

He had been allocated another billet for the new job and again, it turned out to be 'a huge house with a lot of antiques and other valuables.' The owner was Fräulein Michels. Her father, Bowman learned, had been a leading citizen, president of the Chamber of Commerce and a member of the *Bundesrat* [Federal Council]:

Tonight I had another talk with Fräulein Michels and the housekeeper. It was strange to be sitting in a richly furnished room in a mansion talking about the nearness of the owner to starvation. They let me see the fortnightly fat ration for two. It was about what one would put on a plate for tea – I mean the butter or margarine. They are going to show me the weekly ration of meat tomorrow – under ½lb, they say, for the two of them. At the same time I think they are making the most of their sufferings; and I imagine we were a bit worse off in captivity. But as I told you, things are much worse now (at least so they seem to me) than when I was last here. The children, too, are in a bad way. They are getting out of hand. One sees them in a condition of raggedness that was previously almost unknown in Germany.

I came to know of my mysterious correspondent of the other day. It came out quite accidentally when I was talking to Fräulein Michels. She is a rich lady who lives a few doors off. She has three houses in Cöln. But she is a bit crazy, and realising this, the young hooligans have made her the special victim of their pranks. They assemble in front of her house and bait her, throwing stones and breaking her windows – an unheard of thing in Germany! I gave her letter yesterday to Major Osman to read, hardly thinking that he would take it seriously. But he did, and forwarded it to Headquarters.

If it were not for the war embargo on fraternisation, I would have quite a lot of privileges through Fräulein Michels. For instance she would have me meet the director all the museums and picture-galleries here (and Cöln is rich in museums) who would give me any information on anything in his department. As theatre tickets are hard to procure, she has asked me to let her know any time when I want to go, and she will get them for me, as she knows the manager.

Yet while he was enjoying what Cologne had to offer, he had no clear idea regarding how long the army was going to retain him. Time was moving on, and on 4 March Bowman went to the demobilization office to find out when he was likely to be released from the army. The officer in charge was on leave and not due back for a few days. There was a clerk, a private soldier, on duty but he had been in post for only two weeks. He gave Bowman a copy of the regulations to read, and it seemed clear to Bowman that, according to the regulations, he belonged to a class of officer – those with a civilian post overseas – who could not be retained without their consent in the Army of Occupation and who could demand demobilization whenever they wanted it. His case seemed also to be in a category of officer who claimed repatriation at some date ahead. 'So far as I could make out I am absolutely secure – i.e. if the regulations count for anything.'

Then he dropped the bombshell:

> Now, Dearest, suppose the worst came to the worst, and something happened which would make it impossible for me to be demobilized, I want you to face things calmly and with all the bravery which you showed when I went to France. And I want to tell you what I mean to do. I mean first of all to exhaust every possible means to secure my demobilization; and then, failing that, to write to Princeton resigning or offering to resign my chair; and finally, to offer myself for long service (as many years as need be) with the Siberian force. This is part of the official army of occupation, and I daresay it might be possible to get transferred to it by offering to serve for six years or longer. If you want to know why I am thinking of this, I will tell you that since coming to Germany, it has been in my mind a good deal. It is largely the old lure of Russia, and largely the desire to see more active service. And if by a great piece of misfortune I should have to abandon Princeton, it would be necessary to secure a living as far forward as possible, and the army seems the only alternative. Not that I contemplate all this seriously. But we must be prepared for the worst, Dearest; and I would like you to write and let me know what you think of the scheme. It would be a terrible thing living for years apart like this, but with a mutual love and trust like ours, surely all things are possible. Of course Princeton might be willing to wait one more year for me, in which case I'd never think of the other scheme but I don't think that one would be entitled to rely on that.

Was Bowman carried away by his romantic enthusiasm for Russia through its literature, and also for a desire for more active service? He did say that he was not really serious. However, a few days later, in a letter to Kemp Smith, he was even more enthusiastic about the prospect of Russia, should he be forced to remain in the army:

> Should I not be allowed to demobilize, the situation will be serious for me, but I have made up my mind what I shall do. It would hardly be fair to expect Princeton to extend my leave much further; so, if the worst comes to the worst, I shall write Pres. Hibben offering to resign, and if he accepts my resignation, I'll apply for transfer to the Russian force (the Siberian army by preference) on a long-service enlistment. That will secure a livelihood for my family for as long a period as one has any right to look forward to in these days. The distant future will have to look after itself. There are a number of grounds underlying my desire to transfer to Russia. One is my great interest in that country. Another is simply the primitive desire for adventure – a desire which I, as a married man, would not for a moment consider myself justified in entertaining except in so far as I am compelled to remain in the army.

Yet Bowman did not challenge the idea that the army could retain him indefinitely: this was not the age of press gangs; his family had the right of access to a member of parliament; there was scope for political leverage. Surely Princeton's President Hibben – successor to the man who was now president of the United States – could have been asked to write to the United States ambassador to put pressure on the British government for the release of one of the university's professors?

Had he really thought through the consequences for Mabel? The expression 'face things calmly' suggests that he had. She had been broody when Jennie had had a baby the year before, and only wished that she and Bowman could 'have another little chick-a-biddy'. He seems to have taken the view that theirs was a Peter Abélard and Héloïse love, capable of being sustained at a distance.

Part of the difficulty Bowman had, though, was the lack of clarity and guidance on the demobilization procedures. The consensus among the officers he contacted was that it was tricky.

Before the letter even reached Mabel, he followed up the idea with another one: 'However, if anything occurs and I am not able to demobilize at all, I am not worrying about the future. If I can get to Russia it'll mean a great deal. And in a world like this today no one can look far ahead.'

Three days later, he floated another idea:

> Suppose the army plays me false again, and I cannot demobilize, there's a possibility of an alternative scheme to my Russian one; and that is (always supposing the thing becomes possible) that you and the children come out to me here, and that we set up house in Germany for the time being.

***

It was coming up to four years since Mabel had given up a pleasant life at Princeton to return to her parental home to support her husband in fulfilling his duty to his country. All that had happened in those years had taken a toll on her: anxiety about Archie, and running the household with parental disapproval lurking in the background. Archie had come 'marching home again' but it was a short-lived reunion.

Then in 1918 the Great War was superseded by the great flu or 'Spanish flu' pandemic. It raged across the world. Some local communities were worse affected than others. In the Stewart household Johnnie, Mabel and Ian became ill. Johnnie became very ill.

After a few days Mabel began to recover but she was weak. Ian had a temperature. She was too weak to look after the children and there was no possibility of her running the household now, the way she had since Theresa left. 'I'm just going to let things in the household slip. There really is no use my trying to get them into what I consider order. There is too much opposition at headquarters.'

In early March, when she felt stronger, she went to Irvine on the Clyde coast to help out her brother Norman and his wife Margaret who had had a baby. Norman was in the Canadian army and on leave. Mabel took Ian with her; her mother was able to cope with Maisie as she understood her and the pair got along nicely. It was while she was supporting Margaret after the birth of her baby that she got Archie's letter with his idea of volunteering for the expeditionary force to Russia. Its impact on Mabel was hard:

> My own dearest Archie,
>
> I've been getting lots of letters from you recently but my spirits are very low. I shall be so glad when you come home and when we can settle down together. I think dearest my nerve is giving way a bit. If you do think it is your duty to take in the Russia thing Archie I shall endure but just at present I can't face the prospect – even the remotest prospect with any degree of cheerfulness. I was meaning to write you last night dear and consider all the possibilities very carefully but such a terrible

thing happened. I gave our beloved Eenie a teaspoonful of camphorated oil thinking it was olive oil. I discovered the mistake at once and gave him salt and water to make him bring it up but without effect. Then on the nurse's advice I gave him the white of an egg and he swallowed that. The little man seemed not a bit put out with the thing and went off to sleep at once. We all thought he'd be all right but Margaret insisted on Norman going up to the doctor, which he did. She came down about 10 and then we had such a business getting him wakened up and making him sick. The oil had to come up but the doctor didn't want to resort to the stomach pump. The darling boy behaved like the dear wee trump he is and I succeeded in getting him to swallow about a teaspoonful of mustard and water. By tickling his throat the doctor did at last make him vomit and we got it up. I scarcely slept a wink last night beloved I was watching him so carefully. We wheeled the couch into Margaret's room and he lay in it close to me. Through the night he wakened up spontaneously to tell me he loved me, and what a comfort it was to know that he was all right. He's as well as can be today and as bright as ever. O Archie I shudder to think what might have happened to this beloved boy. The doctor doesn't think it would have been fatal but he might have been very ill. I don't know what I should have done dearest. I won't think of it. Thank God the child is all right now but…

She made an effort to move on to other things, wondered if her level of German could be built on in the future as she felt she had a sound foundation, but anxious thoughts returned:

Archie, my own dearest Archie I want you so much but am afraid to have you. Your love is such a wonderful fresh young living thing and Archie I feel so old. The time you have been away seems to have added years to me. It will be different when you come back.

Then the poignant memory of her friend Jennie came to mind, and she asked if he had seen Harry Mackay. She ended her letter: 'Goodnight my best beloved.'

During this trying time, Mabel got support from Norman Kemp Smith. He was in the process of giving up the temporary accommodation he had in London, and moving to Edinburgh to be with his wife before they left for Princeton, so Bowman sent his letters to him via Mabel.

With his experience of working in a government bureaucracy, and with contacts in the War Office, Kemp Smith took a hard-headed line with the idea that Archie could be held by the army indefinitely:

Dear Mrs Bowman

    Many thanks for sending me on Archie's very interesting letter to me. I sincerely hope that he will get teaching work until July and then demobilisation. The latter he <u>must</u> get. His suggestion of enlisting and spending 10 years soldiering in the occupied area is preposterous. The life, especially under such conditions, would surely be bound to become intolerable, and that very speedily. I must write to him tomorrow.

Archie's response to Mabel's news about her mistake in giving Ian camphorated oil arrived. He sidestepped any thought that his proposing to join the Russian expeditionary force might have contributed to distracting Mabel when she was getting Ian ready for bed, but the news had a powerful impact on him:

My Own Darling Wife, my heart almost ceased to beat when I got your letter today telling me about our wee boy's accident. And oh how thankful I am to know that he is all right now. I am so sorry, Beloved, for you; because I realise what it must have meant to you, and what an experience it must have been. I think, Beloved, the strain of this last year has been too much for you; and it's no wonder after all you've come through, that you feel as if you were near the breaking point… So bear up, Dear Lass! The last lap I am sure has come; and then no more parting and roaming if <u>I</u> can help it. And <u>should</u> the worst come, and a long period of separation lies before us – well, Beloved, think what might have been – what nearly <u>was</u>.

However, by now Mabel was resolved in her mind. She wrote:

I shall be eagerly awaiting your decision about your work. I think you took the proper line this time dearest. Dearest when you disapprove I feel so crushed. It took me quite a while to get over your letter even though it was so kind and loving. Archie I love you altogether and only you – I'm awfully sorry dearest but I just couldn't and indeed can't quite face the thought of a long separation. I know dear how much worse it might have been, how much worse it has been for many and many a one but I can't help the fact.

In the days that followed, she allowed herself to daydream for a moment before returning to the practical. If they did ever move to Germany as a family, it would be

a wonderful opportunity for the children to get a mastery over a foreign language. I'd like it to be German too, Germany has meant so much to you

> and the language is so rich in expression. It would be a great experience for all of us but I don't expect it is the least likely to come off. You'll get your demobilization all right and we'll be preparing for Princeton. It is going to be such a wrench to go away this time Archie. I don't like to think of it.

She was wearying to have him home so that they could take up life as a family again:

> I'm just terribly fond of the children Archie. Children are very satisfactory things to a woman like me and your children my dearest are just infinitely dear. They simply reign in everyone's affections. I want you to be with them all the time and watch the unfolding of our little blossoms.

Since February Mabel had been handling correspondence from publishers, passing letters to Archie and taking action herself where she could. When he had been on leave in January, Bowman had begun the search for a publisher for his volume of sonnets. At this stage he had given it the provisional title of *Sonnets Written in Captivity*, and in his covering letter he offered to make a financial contribution to the project. By the time responses came in, he was back on duty in Germany. One early rejection came from a publishing house that felt 'in spite of the evident merit of the work' it was unlikely to sell, notwithstanding the fact 'that Lieut Bowman kindly offered to guarantee us against loss.'

However, two weeks later, John Lane at The Bodley Head confirmed that they would like to publish the collection. Letters between John Lane and Bowman crossed, and on 21 March John Lane wrote again reiterating that he had 'offered to undertake the publication of your book without financial assistance from you. But, on the other hand, if you are in a position to do so, a contribution towards advertising would be of considerable assistance...' and he suggested something in the region of £25 or £50.

They discussed this back and forth by mail and John Lane at one point came back to Bowman thanking him for 'your candid letter of March 29th.' He would carry out 'the prosaic pushing of your poetry' and it would be a help to have 'some sort of guarantee, however small, to fall back on.' Publication got under way, and at the proof stage John Lane wrote to Bowman on 20 May:

> I have read your little volume of poems *Written in Captivity* with great interest, and should be prepared to undertake the whole expenses of publication if you would be content to accept a royalty after 1,000 copies have been sold in which case I should offer you a royalty of 10% on the

2nd 1,000, 12½ on the 3rd.... I may mention that curiously I have recently accepted another volume of poems under the title of *Poems in Captivity*. I think therefore that if you accept my offer it will be necessary to find a slightly different title and I would suggest *Sonnets of a Prisoner*.

He ended with a PS: 'I've been thinking too that some sort of figurative title might be better for the volume, but I don't know I like "Sonnets" in the title don't you?'

When Kemp Smith heard of it, he wrote to Mabel: 'It is splendid news that John Lane has accepted his Sonnets for publication. Lane is a good publisher to have for a volume of this kind.'

Mabel had her own idea about John Lane's suggested title and she wrote to Archie: 'About the title, you will have to think of a title. I didn't like "prisoner" coming in but *Sonnets from a Prison Camp* might be all right.' So this became the title of the book.

***

Archie Bowman hardened his attitude against staying in the army and relegated his *idée fixe* of the Russian expedition to a pipedream. He had an interview with the demobilization officer and was advised to put in for immediate demobilization, not to request it for July. The officer warned him of the old adage that the more time they had to think about it, the less good were the chances. Certainly Bowman found that the army regulations for demobilization were impenetrable; as he told Kemp Smith: 'Demobilization is a process whose mysteries are almost as inscrutable as the mystery of life.' He learned that there was the danger of compulsory retention, and if Princeton had been a Canadian university the army had the means of negotiating to retain him for a year. So he set the process in train.

In the meantime, though, another procedure he had gone through came to its resolution. A repatriated prisoner of war had to make a statement concerning the details of how he came to be taken prisoner. Bowman had furnished his account, and in the fullness of time, in his case 9 April, he received a letter from the Standing Committee at the War Office saying that 'his statement regarding the circumstances of his capture by the enemy having been investigated, the Council considers that no blame attaches to him in this matter.'

As Kemp Smith sent him missives from Warren Fite, chairman of the Philosophy Department, with suggestions for their lecture programme for the following academic year, Bowman got drawn in to planning. He was agreeable to Fite's suggestion that he resign Advanced Logic in the meantime and stick to Greek philosophy. Bowman was happy with the idea; he told Kemp Smith that he wanted to concentrate on Plato and Aristotle for the next twelve years.

Until there was some response to his application for demobilization, Bowman concentrated on his work. He was carrying more and more of the load of interviewing civilians and it was demanding, constantly making decisions with the individual face-to-face with him:

> Today young Baron Oppenheim (they are the great people about here) tried to use his blandishments on me in order to get a pass without the usual formalities. I sent him packing to get his place in the seething mob that daily fights around our premises for admission. Later he sent a message asking for another interview, but I refused to see him. Don't think on this account that I am either a stony-hearted monster or a model of even-handed justice. I am neither the one nor the other; but I have a strong objection to people trying to shove in before the poor widow because their wealth and position make it easier for them to break through the German cordon that keeps the mob at bay.

The word had got about that Bowman's predecessor in the post tended to be a bit lenient with the ladies, but Bowman determined that it would not happen on his watch:

> What amazing people I meet – titled millionaires…blandishing women. You've no idea how they try to work their sex – they come in dressed to kill and overflowing with blandishments and often with all the genius of skilled coquettes. With me it is fatal. To coquettes I am always as hard as stone. Poor simple people I always like to help.

From the beginning of his posting to the permit office he had been on good terms with Fräulein Michels, owner of the mansion in which he was billeted; each respected the other's position, but then the army changed the arrangement and allocated more men to the billet. These men came to expect to be waited on, with the additional food allowance provided by the military. This was a great strain for both Fräulein Michels and Fräulein Sibilla. Bowman sympathized with them and told Fräulein Michels to get a doctor's certificate

> which she can honestly do as both she and Sibilla have been ill… The rest I mean to undertake for them. What I mean to do is to go to the Town Major and try and have the house listed as a billet for one officer only. They want an officer or perhaps two, as protection. I don't know whether the Town Major will take a favourable view of the case. He is a notorious leader of public anti-German propaganda. But in any case it's worth trying.

Digging in. Bowman's early military training, anticipating a war to come. *(Glasgow University Archive)*

The elegant new Clyde-built liner SS *Tuscania* in 1915, on which Archie, Mabel and baby son crossed the Atlantic so that Archie could enlist in the British Army. *(Glasgow University Archive)*

Pre-war days at Princeton, and the young married couple Archie and Mabel Bowman at their first home. *(Glasgow University Archive)*

Tuscania's Captain Peter Maclean showed a high profile on the promenade deck, helping to reassure passengers who feared the 'U-boat terror'. Here he poses holding baby Ian Bowman to have a photo taken. *(Glasgow University Archive)*

Bowman commissioned in the HLI.
(Glasgow University Archive)

Bowman with his son Ian in 1917, before he was sent to France.
(Lydia Bowman collection)

Group of training officers. Bowman centre, second row. *(Glasgow University Archive)*

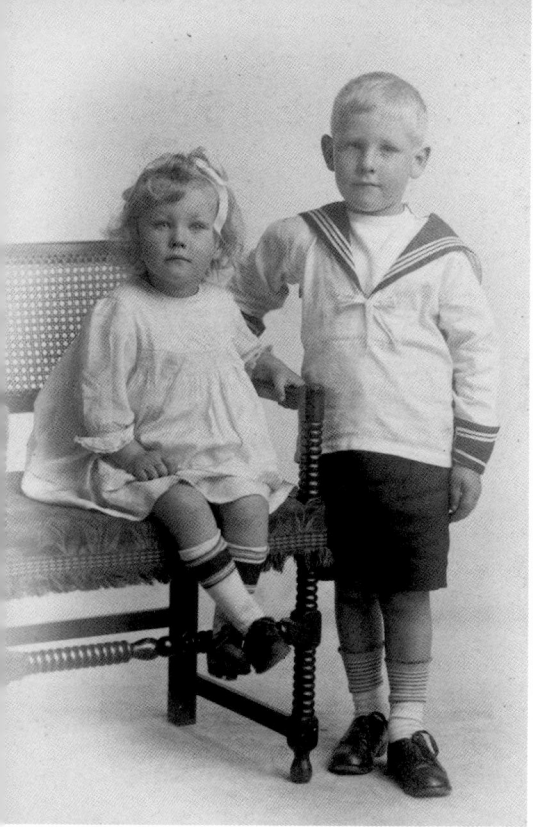

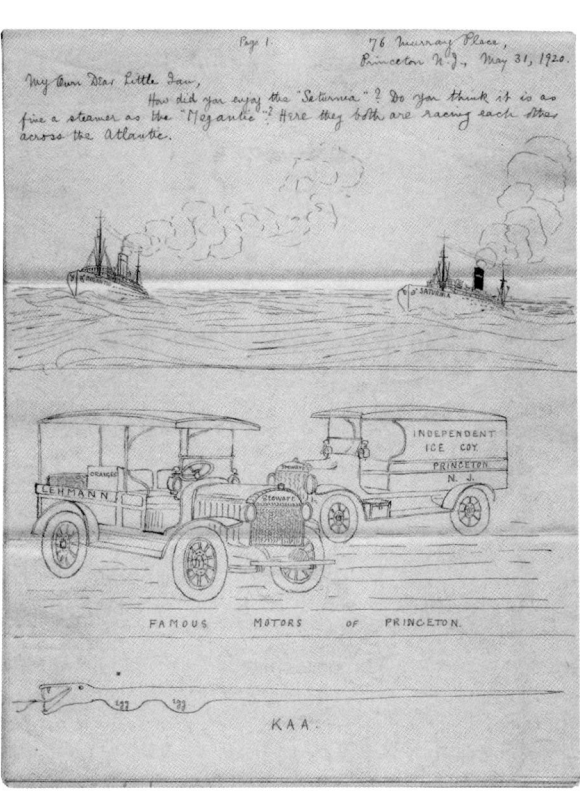

Maisie and Ian — their father in his letters from prison camp wonders if they will remember him. *(Marjorie Stewart collection)*

Page 1.

76 Murray Place,
Princeton N.J., May 31, 1920.

My Own Dear Little Ian,
How did you enjoy the "Saturnia"? Do you think it is as fine a steamer as the "Megantic"? Here they both are racing each other across the Atlantic.

Bowman's drawing for five-year-old Ian. *(Lydia Bowman collection)*

'Where April stirs along Loch Lomond side'. Bowman's reverie just before C Company 10/11th HLI was bombarded at the battle of the Lys. *(David Upton collection)*

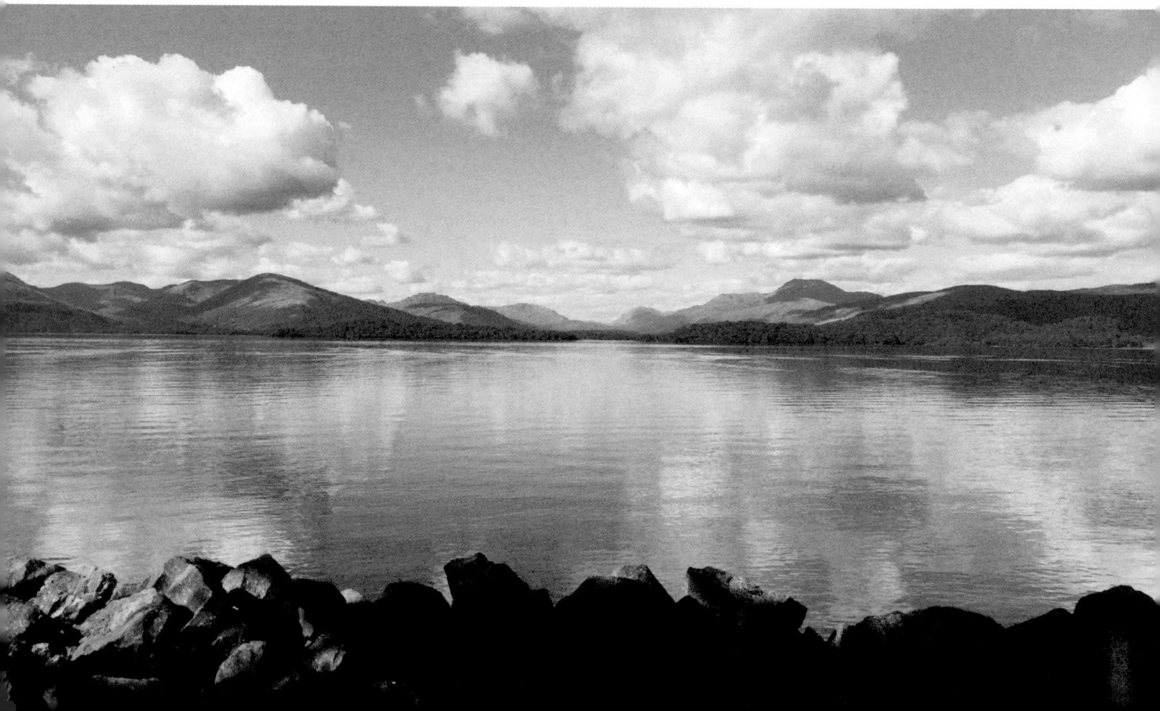

A mixed group of British, French and Portuguese prisoners. *(Bundesarchiv-Bildarchiv)*

Rastatt Prison Camp early in the war. *(Bundesarchiv-Bildarchiv)*

A compound at Rastatt Prison Camp. *(Bundesarchiv-Bildarchiv)*

Professor Archie Bowman, holder of the Stuart Chair of Logic at Princeton. *(Princeton University Archive)*

Mabel Bowman, beloved wife of Archie. *(Marjorie Stewart collection)*

The war is over but Bowman is not yet demobilised. He is at the seaside with Mabel, Ian and Maisie, and Maisie has brought a friend. *(Glasgow University Archive)*

Bowman as guest of honour at the Perth Burns Club, 1933. *(Glasgow University Archive)*

Bowman and his family at Greenock in 1929, on board ship bound for Montreal, from where he would travel across America for his sabbatical at Berkeley. *(Marjorie Stewart collection)*

Maisie Gillespie, early in the Second World War; she did voluntary work driving an ambulance. *(Marjorie Stewart collection)*

Archie Bowman and his colleague Charles Hendel with their families on holiday, 1925. *(Marjorie Stewart collection)*

Flying Officer Alastair Bowman; he did not survive the war. *(Marjorie Stewart collection)*

Ian Bowman, who did so much to preserve his father's legacy. *(Marjorie Stewart collection)*

Squadron Leader Robert Gillespie. *(Marjorie Stewart collection)*

Professor Norman Kemp Smith; Archie Bowman's great friend and supporter. *(Edinburgh University Archive)*

In the background, the allies were determining the scale of reparations that Germany would have to make for the war. Speculation was rife in the officers' mess about what was necessary and there the mood was to squeeze Germany 'till the pips squeak'. The German people waited to hear what other heavy burdens they would have to bear as well as blame for the war.

Bowman got out and among people as much as he could, and on May Day he stood and watched a socialist parade:

> It was a pouring wet day, and everybody carried umbrellas. The faces were sad and cheerless. Enormous numbers of women and children marching in the ranks, young lads and girls arm in arm, old women, cripples – everybody well-clad, many in their old war uniforms (probably their only suits). The bands all had tiled hats, as had many of the processors. They came by trades or societies, each with its banner or placard; and there were many miscellaneous placards bearing mottos such as *Gleiches Recht für alle* [Equal Rights for all]… The waiters were a remarkable group – spotlessly arrayed even on this wet, muddy day. Though they were buttoned up one could see their perfectly laundered collars. Evidently they had made it a point of honour to maintain their best professional get-up. What struck me was the comparative absence of British soldiers. Hardly any came in sight, and except for an occasional mounted man, there was no evidence of policing at all. I am so glad. It was so magnificently British not to intrude our arrangements, and to trust the people. They certainly well-earned our trust, for a more orderly mob you couldn't find anywhere. My heart went out to these poor people, and I had moments of keen realisation of what Christ must have felt where it is said He pitied the people when they appeared to Him as sheep having no shepherd. One small incident jarred me. Outside the *Apostelkirche* right in front of me was a little group – a girl of perhaps 12 or 13 and two little children, whose happy laughter rang out all the time. Beside us was a pale, solemn-faced little man, who took the children to task for laughing in the old German fashion so characteristic of the people. It makes me feel that underneath the magnificently regimented life, was a bad spirit which began by throttling the innocent upwelling of the child's soul and would end by binding the citizen body <u>and</u> soul.

During the spring months, Bowman and Kemp Smith shared their thoughts about the future of Germany. The terms of the peace treaty were now known, and Kemp Smith felt they were severe. Bowman felt they were severe but not too severe. He had great sympathy for the people, but he felt that neither the war nor the German people had succeeded in overthrowing the ruling elite of Imperial Germany:

> As yet it looks to me as if the only people who can govern Germany are the evil class that governed it before and during the war; and it is to prevent the country falling back in its helplessness and weariness into the clutches of this alert and cynical monster that we must keep our stranglehold un-relaxed for a long time to come.

It was the case that in the aftermath of war the power of the industrialists and the landowners was unbroken. Bowman outlined his thinking to Kemp Smith at length:

> The European situation is more bewildering than ever. I should greatly like to know whether the Paris potentates expect the Germans to sign the peace conditions. The more I accumulate impressions the more I feel that Germany has not been sufficiently castigated. At first it was a little difficult to resist the inflow of friendly feeling, where one was greeted by such super-abounding kindness as we are here; but I have had time to see the moving of sinister forces behind the surface. It isn't that I think our hosts are either acting a servile part or are trying to deceive us. Their kindness (which is little short of a scandal) is really genuine; and I think wherever direct human relations are concerned the German is at his best. But I find it difficult to resist the conclusion that the erstwhile governing classes in the country are now as ever without honour or conscience in public matters; and the feeling grows daily stronger that the only hope of Germany is the effectual subjugation of this class. At present it is only lying low – and not too low either; and what I am afraid of is that the moderate party of progress will not be strong enough to keep it under. The progress of the revolution has been most disappointing; and although it may seem a monstrous thing to say, I cannot help hoping, for the sake of the German people themselves, that the worst is still to come. The inertia to be overcome before anything permanent can be effected is simply incalculable, and it is difficult to see where the dislodging force is to come from if it does not come from the Spartacists. I have the feeling very strong that the day for wise counsels and moderation has no more dawned for the world than it had when every consideration for historical precedent had to give place to the desperate devices of the war. I should think otherwise if I saw Germany salted with fire as Russia has been salted. Short of that I have not very much hope, though there

is sometimes a danger of failing to realize how near at hand salvation may be. It is to be hoped that it may be nearer in this case than seems likely at present. I must confess, one of the disquieting thoughts that haunts my mind is the suggestion that perhaps the master spirit of the age, the real <u>carrier</u> of history, will turn out not to be President Wilson but Trotsky. If that should prove to be so (which God forbid), I should not even then for a moment despair of the world, but should take the portent as the measure of the world's rottenness before the war, and of the extent to which we have still to revise our estimate of the whole situation. A thing I can never get out of my mind is the fact that while we went to war with a weak country like China in order to compel her to take our soul-destroying opium; while we were willing to endanger the peace of Europe (that holy of holies in whose name we have always justified our connivance at international crime) with our Boer war, – while we did these things because monetary interests were at stake, we allowed the Armenians and the Bulgarians to be massacred by their hundreds of thousands, we shut our eyes to the Congo atrocities and actually courted the friendship of official Russia. In view of facts like these (and I think they are symptomatic of our whole national life in one of its aspects) I don't think we should have any cause to complain should Bolshevism come to scour and scald us as it is scouring and scalding Russia today. At the thought of such a possibility, while the family man within me grows sick with fear, the unregenerate Adam rises up with all the exhilaration born of an ineradicable love of destruction – which after all is a vital thing and very necessary. You may gather from this that I am still in the deep and I do not feel (or sense) ground anywhere. Until I do so I am not likely to feel any enthusiasm for restructuring, or anything more than the weariness of the natural man for a settled life. To put it bluntly, if there is still a lot of fighting to be done, I'd like to be where the fighting is; and in going forward with my efforts towards demobilization I must confess I suffer many a pang to be with the little Russian expeditionary force. The strongest (personal) desire of all, however, is to be back to philosophy.

While he looked forward to going back to philosophy, Bowman's usefulness to the army was working against his own interests. The army badly wanted to keep him on in the role he had, and Captain Garratt, his immediate boss, went behind Bowman's back to do the groundwork for a scheme to hold on to him. On 6 May, Garratt told him that that he had to report to the general that day but to go first to Captain Osman. Then Garratt told him part of the ploy: he had gone to the American army liaison officer, Colonel Biddel, for advice on how best to keep

Bowman. The liaison officer suggested that the general should cable President Hibben and ask for Bowman's release for another year. 'I said nothing, but I was a bit worried as you can imagine, and made up my mind that nothing would keep me in the army if anything I could do would prevent it.'

Yet could he prevent it? He presented himself at headquarters and first met Captain Osman, who told him that a letter had been written about him to the general. Bowman knew nothing about it and said so. Osman had assumed the letter had been written with Bowman's consent and gave it to him to read. Basically, the letter described Bowman as a hard-working officer who knew his own mind and understood how to handle the Germans and if he demobilized, they did not know how he would be replaced. Osman also confirmed the idea of sending a cable to Princeton. The general was at a meeting and Bowman was told to return at 3.00 pm.

At the appointed time Bowman presented himself. The general had a staff colonel with him; they both told him how useful he had been to them and they did not know how he could be replaced. 'But I said that under no circumstances would I consent to remain in the army, and the general at once said that if that was so, that was an end of the matter.' When Bowman returned to the permit office and reported the outcome, he expected a scene with Garratt but his boss took it well and recommended Bowman's discharge.

For the next two weeks, Archie Bowman was demob-happy, attending the theatre as often as possible, catching up on everything he could. He wanted to share his joy with Mabel; he wanted to discuss Hermann Sudermann's play *Johannisfeuer* [*Fires of St John*] with her as he thought it was a masterpiece; the role of the heroine one of the greatest 'female creations of literature'. His thoughts went back to their past young life and a phantasy thought of a future:

> should it ever be our fortune to live together in Germany we will have everything in common. For you as for me Germany will be a land of romance and joy, a great humanity over which a dark cloud fell. It would be in vain to deny it – Germany has exercised and exercises a spell over my mind. It was the country we always looked to together as the scene of our romance; and though nothing on earth could have exceeded that one night we had, we will still look to Germany as a land of pilgrimage. How it of all lands has severed us, Beloved. How it has been bound up with our destiny.

He went to see Georg Kaiser's *Die Versuchung* [*The Temptation*] twice. This was because of the actress Elsa Baumbach: he thought her acting was sincere and impressive; she looked so plain and simple but her acting was electrifying.

In the meantime, Princeton Philosophy was preparing the timetable and teaching schedule for the new session. Warren Fite, chairman of the Philosophy Department, did not have Bowman's address and sent his proposals for him to Kemp Smith:

> You will note that for the second term we have boldly put Bowman down for French Philosophy. I have asked you to negotiate that point with Bowman. I enclose two copies of the program in order that you may send him one. I hope that he may take the appointment as a stimulus if he is not already prepared. There will be time before the second term. I shall be glad to hear from you about this when you have heard from him.

***

Mabel had already been planning for their return to Princeton and she made the decision to take the lease of a house that Bowman's colleague Charles Hendel was giving up. It was a suitable size for a family and in an attractive part of Princeton. This would be the second time of setting up their own home, and when she was writing to tell Archie about it, her mind went back to when they first started going out together:

> that strange, shy, weird expectant feeling of that first walk comes over me. I am so happy my beloved that you loved me then. I loved you too dear, I think there never was a time when I didn't love you. I think I knew from the first moment that I had power over you and could make you mine. What a long, long walk it was that first night and it wasn't half long enough. All the years that have passed haven't been half long enough either. I think we could walk on for ever together and still be unsatisfied.

In early May, Mabel took a trip by steamer to Tighnabruaich. This was where she and Jennie had often come together. It was only six months since the latter had died; it was here that Mabel knew she was still grieving for Jennie and it stayed with her. She told Archie:

> Dearest I've been thinking about our Jennie all the time today. A year ago she was staying here with us and now she is gone. The children still remember her and talk of her sometimes. Apart from America Jennie seems to have been all mixed up in our lives. At Tighnabruaich I could have wept, she seemed so near. I seemed to see her waiting for me outside

at almost every one of the familiar shops. I could almost hear the snatches of music that I knew were passing through her mind. Even the little ice cream shop holds many a memory. And yet dearest I can scarcely move a finger to get in touch with those who were near to her. Even the baby seems a stranger. I must look up my letters to you and find out exactly what we did a year ago this Sunday. I remember the Saturday party, the fun and hilarity in the drawing room. *Three Blind Mice* was sung with great éclat and at the height of the din who should come in but father's cousin Andrew Stewart and his wife. They had recently lost their only son and I felt so ashamed of our hilarity in the face of their grief. Sunday seems to me to have been a warm and quiet sort of day nothing special doing and Jennie to my disappointment went away early in the forenoon to get Cathie's dinner ready. O my Archie I'm sorry to write to you sadly but I know you are altogether in sympathy with me in this. Dearest I feel her death more than ever. I'm glad she meant so much to you too and that you understand. And now, my beloved, good night. I love you more than ever and long for you utterly.

As the days and weeks before demobilization crawled by, Archie found the strain of the workload getting to him. He told Kemp Smith about it:

The strain of life and work here is excessive and I am very tired. I find personal interviews (my special business, I do the interviews for the whole place) very trying. One has to go through so many scenes. One of the worst features is the constant struggle against feminine influence. The Permit Office is a great centre for that kind of pressure. Another worry is the struggle against our own and French officers (often of higher rank) who come to try and extort privileges for female protégés. Only a few days ago one of our officers brought up a French general to work me on behalf of some woman. I refused and kept my position intact against their pressure; but that sort of thing takes it out of one. At present we are having a regular death-struggle with a prominent Cabaret. We have refused to allow the artists whom they have engaged to travel in, and they are bringing great pressure to bear through officers of ours. Finally they have managed to enlist a staff officer who is threatening to lay the matter before the army commander. I could ask for nothing better; but I imagine if Sir William Robertson is invoked, the bolt may rebound on the heads of our opponents. One thing gives us an enormous pull and makes our position almost impregnable. That is the fact that they are in desperate straits for officers with a sufficient knowledge of Germany to do the work.

In mid-May Mabel wrote to Archie, enclosing a newspaper cutting reporting the retirement of Professor Pringle-Pattison who held the Chair of Moral Philosophy at Edinburgh University.

Bowman wrote at once to Kemp Smith: 'I have hardly any doubt that you will be his successor.' In his enthusiasm he wrote as though it was all signed and sealed: 'I know of many who will rejoice with me to see you in Scotland again, and I know of one who will rejoice in an extreme degree. That is Dixon; though I think he would fain have you in Glasgow.' However, he envisaged the knock-on effect in that he and Mabel would find it a great loss when they returned to Princeton.

Then, out of the blue, on 21 May he was told that he could clear his desk and prepare for departure. He went back to his sumptuous billet, to the place that had been home for three months, went down to the kitchen and told the housekeeper Fräulein Sibilla that he was demobilizing in a few days and asked if he could get a box in which to pack his books. 'She was greatly moved at the news and tears came into her eyes; but I comforted her by telling her I would try and get a good man in my place.'

However, true to army tradition, the next day the potential for Sod's law to apply came into play when Bowman found that there was still one final hurdle: the adjutant general had the final disposal of all German-speaking officers in his hands and his consent was necessary before Bowman could be demobbed. He had his case made out: he had a letter from President Hibben of Princeton University and a letter from Warren Fite on the programme and the lectures Bowman would take in the Philosophy Department. He thought his case almost impregnable.

On 25 May he knew his demobilization had cleared all hurdles and in a matter of days he would be on his way. He told Mabel: 'It's almost like a dream – the unrealizable thing it seemed before our marriage – that we should be absolutely together again.'

Finally, five days later, his dispersal certificate was signed and he was on his way home.

***

Two weeks later, with Mabel and the children on holiday at West Kilbride, Bowman wrote a testimonial in support of Kemp Smith's application for the chair of Moral Philosophy at Edinburgh University. Bowman wrote Kemp Smith to make any alteration (with any adjustment of phrase the sequence may demand):

> 'I attach special importance to Prof Kemp Smith's remarkable powers as a teacher. At Princeton he has been long accustomed to deal with very large classes, and to carry these along with him by the sheer force and charm of a personality which seems to invest everything it touches with an

> immediate and sustained interest. I have never once known the problem of discipline even to arise in any course for which Prof Kemp Smith was responsible.' (Perhaps the word 'even' might be omitted from the last sentence. I am sorry I could hardly address the testimonial 'Cologne' as it was thought out as well as written on my return to Glasgow. I think, however, as I am still in the service and have no knowledge of my being as yet struck off the strength of my branch, you could safely address 'General Headquarters, British Army of the Rhine.'
>
> I hope these suggestions will effect the improvement you have in view. To be quite candid, it never occurred to me that a testimonial from me would have the slightest value to you, and I never thought of writing one from Cologne, or indeed until Mabel got Mrs Kemp Smith's letter. The one unhappy feature in our relations has always been that I never felt able to compete with you in mutual services. It has therefore come as a very pleasant surprise that you should consider anything I can say of even infinitesimal value to you.

Bowman could not resist telling Kemp Smith about Macneile Dixon's enthusiasm to see him being appointed at Edinburgh; he told him that Dixon said to him 'that it "would be a great day for Scotland" when you were safely seated in the chair.'

Within two weeks, Bowman was writing to him again:

> the great and glad news reached me too late tonight to reply to you by telegraph. Mabel and I are overjoyed, and for the present we won't allow our joy to be in any way marred by selfish thoughts of what we personally are losing. It's truly magnificent – exactly the place one would have chosen for you if one had the disposal of people's destinies in one's hands. Will you convey my heart-felt congratulations to Mrs Kemp Smith. I should like to congratulate Edinburgh if one knew how to perform such a feat; and I rejoice that what Dixon described as 'a great day for Scotland' has really come.

As for Bowman, four years after he left the US to join the British army, he reported to Pirbright Repatriation Centre to be given warrants for berths for his family on the SS *Megantic* sailing on 12 September from Liverpool to Montreal. From Montreal, they would go on by rail to New Jersey.

Of the three British academics (referred to in the *New York Times*) who were released from Princeton to serve their country, one gave his life for it, one remained behind in it to fulfil a distinguished career, and the third returned to Princeton a bigger man.

Chapter Six

Princeton

A man's personality must make its appeal here.
Archie Bowman

Right from the start of his second stint at Princeton, Bowman's teaching sparkled. Although the Philosophy Department was in the doldrums and its student numbers overall were down, enrolments for his courses on Greek Philosophy and Hegel's Logic increased; at the end of his one-term Fundamental Problems course, which had doubled in size, he had a deputation of students wanting to continue it without credit. Since that was not possible, they constituted themselves as the Princeton Philosophical Club, and (after he borrowed enough chairs) they met in his house on Wednesday evenings, their sessions often lasting till midnight. As a result of its success, the following year his colleague, Charles Hendel, organized a group of the sophomores into a philosophical society, so there were two undergraduate philosophical societies, both going concerns. Bowman also began to be in great demand to give public lectures that soon had to be held in the largest halls at the university.

His book of sonnets was on sale in the university bookstore, and Le Secrétaire Général of the BIBLIOTHÈQUE ET MUSÉE DE LA GUERRE in Paris wrote to him via his publisher requesting a copy for its English Language section on books on the war, adding: 'Should you have other publications either on the war or on subjects related to it, or on peace problems and reconstruction, I shall be grateful if you will include them.'

So the war had certainly changed him, but he was finding that it had changed America too. 'America is a queer place for a Britisher to live in these days,' he confided to Kemp Smith. There was a growing resentment against the Old World, and 'large elements in America are repenting that they took any part in the war.'

In June that year, the leaders of the allies – Britain, France, Italy and the United States – had agreed on the terms of the Treaty of Versailles that included President Woodrow Wilson's 'Fourteen Points', a statement of principles for world peace. Point XIV included the setting up of a League of Nations: 'A general association of nations must be formed under specific covenants for the purpose of affording mutual guarantees of political independence and territorial integrity to great and small states alike.'

As far as the United States was concerned, however, before the treaty could be accepted, it had to be ratified by Congress. The Senate was split on this issue, and in November the Senate majority leader, who opposed the treaty, tabled an amended version of Wilson's 'Fourteen Points' which watered down the influence that a League of Nations could have on the United States. It went to the vote: President Wilson's supporters opposed that version and it failed to get the required two-thirds majority. Then a second vote was taken without the reservations and it too failed to get the two-thirds majority.

So Bowman felt bleak about the American political system. He took the view that there was a flaw in the structure: the separation of the executive and the legislature, he felt, was a mistake. He also thought that when the presidency was effectually held, as it was with Wilson, 'the President seems invariably to go out under a cloud and to be lost to the public service.'

For a while, he felt that the Senate did not represent the mood in the country as a whole and that a reaction could set in. In January, he wrote:

> Opinion in America seems to me to be growing against the attitude of the Senate. In fact the Senate is a widely discredited institution. Some 300 universities and colleges, including the big ones, took a straw vote on the Treaty a few days ago. The result was a big majority for immediate ratification and a very large vote for ratification without reservations.

However, the student vote did not reflect political opinion. The Senate took a final vote on the treaty on 19 March 1920 and it suffered the same fate. Next day the *New York Times* reported: 'After the session ended senators of both parties united in declaring that in their opinion the treaty was now dead to stay dead.'

Woodrow Wilson's time as a great leader had passed. Insiders who knew him from his Princeton days were saying that Wilson had had a stroke but it was being hushed up. With the lack of a strong executive, it seemed to Bowman that America would not play a positive role in creating a stable post-war world. Congress, he thought, was no more 'capable of conducting the business of foreign affairs than a school of monkeys.'

Campus life, though, had not changed much in his absence for Princeton held still a centuries-old protestant ethos that issued from its presidency. Two Scottish presidents of the university had left their imprint: the eighteenth-century clergyman/politician John Witherspoon, a Founding Father of the United States and signatory of the Declaration of Independence; and the nineteenth-century philosopher and theologian James McCosh, one of the first clergymen in America to argue that Darwinism was not inconsistent with the handiwork of a divine Creator. True, in the early twentieth century, Woodrow Wilson, during his presidency of the university, slightly dented its WASP casing by admitting Jewish and Catholic students (but still not African-American students); then after his tenure came Presbyterian minister John Hibben.

Still, times were a-changing: it was the start of the jazz age and there were Dionysian scenes at the 1920 Junior Prom when students bussed in hookers from New York. Even although he had been a wartime soldier, Bowman drew a puritanical line here, writing of 'girls and men alike intoxicated and women of a low character imported from New York.'

Although the classroom was vibrant with the excitement of ideas, he found the department dispiriting: its tone had changed during the four years he had been away. 'You are very badly missed, and we can never hope to fill your place,' Bowman told Kemp Smith. However, that was what Bowman felt, not his colleagues. There was in-fighting about who should occupy the McCosh Chair of Philosophy that Kemp Smith had held and that spilled over into feeling against the two who held titular chairs: Bowman and Warren Fite, 'both interlopers promoted over the heads of locals.' The upshot was that President Hibben postponed making the appointment.

Also things did not go well at the interpersonal level. To begin with, Bowman's relations with Warren Fite, chairman of the Philosophy Department, were good: Bowman liked him and respected his intellectual strengths, but felt he was very 'doctrinaire and negative and cynical', not traits that Bowman thought would contribute much to teaching moral philosophy. Bowman's method of coping with him was to listen to him giving vent to his views but make no comment on them. This tactic worked well enough for a few months but then, after what seemed like a good idea at the time, a situation developed that led to open hostility.

The Bowmans were in the house on Murray Place that Mabel had leased when Archie was stationed in Cologne. However, after one year in it, and with two young children, they thought they would look for something bigger. Warren Fite and his family leased a house on Fitz Randolph Road, and he told Bowman that he was giving up the lease at the end of session because it was an intolerable burden. Immediately Bowman asked him if he minded his putting in a request to take up the lease when it became available; that way he would be first in line for it. There was no problem with that, but the owner wanted Bowman to take on a five-year lease. At that, Mabel came up with the idea – 'half-jocularly' – that, when they moved in, the Fite family could stay on in the house with them 'and Fite snatched at it eagerly.' Bowman had reservations: 'though such experiments are fraught with risk, and Fite is just the sort of person who creates difficulties through temperamental eccentricities, I have a good deal of confidence in Mabel's capacity to put the thing through and make it a success.' So in the fall of 1920, both families shared a house on Fitz Randolph Road.

At first, Bowman told Kemp Smith, the relations between both families were 'all that could be desired', though Bowman saw from early on that Fite

> cannot be treated as a sane and normal individual. When we describe a man as 'not himself', we usually think of some occasional aberration; but it is only occasionally that Fite is 'himself'. He suffers from chronic irritability, which vents itself in unrestrained ravings, which he is capable of keeping up for hours.

How Mabel and Archie handled such sessions was to let him go on and on but make no comment or treat the thing as a joke.

Nevertheless, the house-sharing arrangement broke up in acrimony before the academic year was out. Bowman found out that Fite was badmouthing Mabel 'to every casual acquaintance' and he tackled him on it – in the presence of Mabel – and gave him a choice: 'I had to demand an apology from him for my wife on the threat of immediate ejection from the house if he refused. He complied but at the same time broke off all personal relations with us.' So by the end of May 1921, both families were living under the same roof 'but as complete strangers.' The rift was also carried over into their working life: Fite would not deal directly with Bowman but only through a departmental colleague, Charles Hendel. Bowman explained to Kemp Smith: 'the thing that is driving him to distraction is that he had to apologise for an offence which he instantly admitted when it was put to him.' What else could I have done in the circumstances, Bowman asked himself, 'unless I had refrained from giving him a chance and given him a beating instead.' Bowman summed up his overall assessment of the man: 'Fite has fine qualities and splendid powers, but everything has been sacrificed to an egotism that is now little short of a mania.'

However, it stressed Bowman having to do this in his home with his wife a part of it; he suffered chest pains and rapid heartbeat and he thought he was suffering heart failure. It turned out to be stress-related, 'but it seemed to me at the time to be the end of me.'

He had done it, though, unflinchingly, for the war had hardened him; he had commanded men and they had stood facing death together. Those years were now slipping into the past, but he had a reminder of them in the spring of that year when he received a letter from a fellow academic, and an honourable man, a former enemy:

> *Professor Hohnholz, Vergesack (Bremen) 19. 2. 21*
> *Verehrter und lieber Herr Professor Bowman!*
> *Durch die freundliche Erwähnung meines Namens im Vorwort zu den „Sonnets from a Prison Camp"...*
> Esteemed and dear Professor Bowman!

You have brought me great joy through the warm mention of my name in the foreword to *Sonnets from a Prison Camp*, and through the sending of a copy of the book and your letter to me, for which I give my heartfelt thanks. In Hesepe I did my duty for you and the other British officers who were interned there as prisoners of war in the struggle for their homeland.

If I, as you put it so graciously in your letter, assisted in the process of 'Germans and the British getting to know each other better and hate and despise each other less', I would consider that the greatest reward. I would have liked to have had a closer relationship with some of you, had the circumstances not been so difficult at the time.

In particular, I would have liked to have had more scholarly discussions with you; I have often wished for that, especially since our academic interests overlap – you are a philosopher and I am a historian and economist.

Perhaps fate is on our side and we will meet again! If you, and I am certain this will be the case, return to Europe and want to take your family on a 'pleasure trip' to explore the place where the camp stood, then write to me, hopefully beforehand and I will be your guide. You and yours can then visit my wife and me here in our home in Vergesack-Bremen. You would be most welcome!

Since the day on which we saw each other last, the day of your departure for Cologne, the political situation has changed dramatically. My homeland, the German Empire, has fallen into a deep crisis. Your homeland, England (and the United States) can be proud of their success in the war.

As you can well imagine, dear Prof. Bowman, as a former Royal Prussian Officer and for a man of my social standing and of my age, in the prime of my life, it is emotionally a difficult task for me to adjust to the dreadfully changed outward circumstances of my beloved homeland, and in these circumstances to find my way. This isn't helpful though, we German men need to find a solution to this difficult task.

As much as I greatly respect my homeland and its devoted people, I have always felt a deep admiration for the greatness of English (and American) culture. As a historian, I have had ample opportunity to present the imposing unity of British politics to other Germans. I have always endeavoured to show my admiration for English politics and culture. How great it is for a people to say: 'Right or wrong, my country' or, 'Britons never will be slaves'!

My country has primarily been destroyed through international Marxism. Social Democracy and Communism will cause us even greater problems still.

The tremendous devaluation of German money has affected us, high-ranking civil servants particularly badly. All the necessities of life are now 20 to 25 times more expensive than before the war, but my salary for example is only 3-4 times higher than before the war. You can easily imagine therefore how much the standard of living has been depressed for me and my circle of friends.

A manual worker earns more today than senior civil servants and professors! In the long term this is naturally an untenable situation. How and when these conditions will change cannot be known in the darkness which hangs over our future. German academics now need to use everything they have and earn just to buy food which is often substandard. Nothing remains for books and travel and so on.

I am glad that I travelled widely before the war in Germany, Austria and Switzerland and that I know Copenhagen, Amsterdam, Brussels, Paris, London, Milan, Rome, Naples and Genoa. That is now a spiritual asset which cannot be taken away from us poor Germans with so few worldly goods.

Otherwise my family and I are well, and I hope this is also the case for you. It would be a great joy if you were also of the opinion that relations between us should remain alive, and that from time to time you demonstrate that with letters – until such time that you and your dear family can come and meet us and be welcomed by us here. I am already excited by the prospect of a quick reply from you and continue to send good wishes.
Your thankful servant,
Prof. Hohnholz

A world war was over and former enemies could communicate, but the blow-up with Fite could not be smoothed over. Fite put about a different story: Bowman had unfairly taken advantage of his lease and threated him with eviction from the house. So tension in the department was part of working life.

When term was over and the marking complete, the Bowmans left for Nova Scotia for the vacation. While they were away, Fite moved his family out of the house.

However, the night before Bowman left for Nova Scotia, President Hibben sent for him and asked him if he would take over the chairmanship of the department. Hibben made it plain that he wanted to get rid of Fite as chairman and at that, Bowman had to bring his problem with Fite into the open and told the president about the complete impasse. If he took over the chairmanship, it would add to his embarrassment. Hibben said that he would do nothing until the autumn to give Bowman time to think it over. Bowman agreed with Hibben, though, that

Fite as chairman was unfortunate for the department; graduate students had been offended by Fite's course on Problems in Philosophy. This was a course that Hibben himself used to give before he became president. Bowman had sat in on Fite's version of the course and felt it was a mistake for him to have it. While 'it was full of cleverness, it was about as undignified as a street-corner oration – a vulgar and malicious attack on the scientists and economists – grossly unfair and about the most scandalous misrepresentation of philosophy I have ever listened to.'

From the president's perspective, though, there was an even more compelling reason to have someone else as chairman of the department: the position carried with it membership of the Advisory Council, which had responsibility for passing all promotions and increases in salary, and in the light of Fite's unpopularity in the faculty, Hibben felt he had to be replaced.

So on 15 June, with that decision suspended, Bowman left Princeton on vacation and to sort out his thoughts. He had quite a lot to think about, as Kemp Smith had written to him before the end of term to say that the chair of Moral Philosophy at Glasgow University would become vacant next year and suggested he apply for it, but at the same time told him that he thought his chances were remote.

Bowman's first response was 'I'm terrified out of my wits by the very thought of anything as honorific as the Glasgow chair.' He had doubts about his readiness for it. One of the penalties attached to having the chair of a department in a Scottish university, he felt, was 'the prominence it gives its holder in the public eye, and the presumption it carries with it that one will assume the manifold functions of a public man as a matter of course.'

So he and Mabel had many evening discussions about where they wanted to be and what would be best for themselves and the children. They came to the provisional decision that Archie should apply when the time came.

In the meantime, they gave themselves up to enjoying the vacation. They were in Nova Scotia as the guests of Ramsay Traquair. He was an Edinburgh man, and he held the Macdonald Chair in Architecture at McGill University. The three had met the previous year on the Atlantic crossing on Mabel and Archie's return from a holiday in Scotland. Traquair had bought an old farmhouse in Guysborough and invited them to spend the vacation there. It was an excellent house, 'roomy and convenient', and there was a little estate as well of hayfields sloping down to the shore and what seemed to Archie like miles of forest behind. The foreshore had a rocky promontory and 'a perfect anchorage'; Traquair's boat had been fitted with a mast and sail, and there was a boathouse.

Bowman described it in terms of an idyll; nature and man in harmony:

> For seven enchanted days we were sailing or otherwise journeying through archipelagos of haunting islands, or along lovely fjords or

across stretches of the open sea, visiting unimaginably picturesque French villages, watching the fishing fleet at their work (swordfish harpooning) or driving along under the shadow of the black Newfoundland mountains or canoeing up a Newfoundland river, spending the night in a village home or in a remote farmhouse or in a little capital city or on board ship... If anything could exceed the beauty of nature in these parts it is the beauty of human nature when left to itself. Here, owing chiefly I think to isolation and the absence of facilities for communication, there still exists a splendidly self-sufficient and reliant population – desperately poor in a monetary sense, yet on the whole sufficiently supplied with what they need in kind. Every woman has her spinning wheel and spins her own wool into thread. Every man can build a house, and a number can build a boat or even a ship. The waterways are crowded with sailing ships, splendid sea-craft, and yet constructed in some clearing of the woods by farmer-fishermen or the miscellaneous craftsmen of the country without the smallest inkling of science but out of a fine sensitiveness for form and proportion bred of experience alone. To see the people work is a tonic in itself. Their courage and cheerfulness and simplicity are most engaging. The very idea of a labour problem would be unintelligible to them, and the conditions of life are such as to call for no social distinctions. Every man is as good as his neighbour not because of any theory of human rights, but because in the nature of things people must all live approximately the same sort of lives. The farmer-fisherman is the type. The citizen is only a slight variant on the latter, for in all likelihood he lays down his tools at 5pm not in order to enjoy the leisure his trade union prescribes for him but in order to start working on his hay – which he will do till 10.30 if the moon is at the full. The road surveyor's cow-bells tinkle along his roads, and his ten-year-old son goes forth each afternoon to drive the cow under some convenient spruce, where he sits down and milks her on the spot. Even the postal authorities are only half-and-half officials and a class apart; and I was amused the other day to hear that the motor which carries the mails and an odd passenger was not available because it was required to transport a load of hay. I feel I am bewitched, and scarcely contemplate a return to the sophisticated society of Princeton without a shudder. If I had the means I'd feel a strong temptation to buy this property and settle down on it for life. Never yet have the conditions been so propitious for my own special work. I can settle down to it with a sustained zest and an enjoyment that could hardly be excelled, and the absence of distractions and interruptions is pure bliss.

Freepost Plus RTKE-RGRJ-KTTX
Pen & Sword Books Ltd
47 Church Street
BARNSLEY
S70 2AS

DISCOVER MORE ABOUT MILITARY HISTORY

Pen & Sword Books have over 4000 books currently available, our imprints include; Aviation, Naval, Military, Archaeology, Transport, Frontline, Seaforth and the Battleground series, and we cover all periods of history on land, sea and air.

Keep up to date with our new releases by completing and returning the form below (no stamp required if posting in the UK).

Alternatively, if you have access to the internet, please complete your details online via our website at **www.pen-and-sword.co.uk**.

All those subscribing to our mailing list via our website will receive a free e-book, *Mosquito Missions* by Martin W Bowman. Please enter code number ACC1 when subscribing to receive your free e-book.

Mr/Mrs/Ms ....

Address.......................

Postcode............... Email address................

Website: www.pen-and-sword.co.uk Email: enquiries@pen-and-sword.co.uk
Telephone: 01226 734555 Fax: 01226 734438
Stay in touch: facebook.com/penandswordbooks or follow us on Twitter @penswordbooks

However, the idyll had to end, and he had to go back to face the fray in the department and cope with the increasing pressures that were brought on by his popularity as an outstanding teacher and a public speaker.

For by now he had become a figure at Princeton. He told Kemp Smith that it was embarrassing: 'I appear to be becoming somewhat of a (local) – well, I don't know how to put it, but it amounts to this, that I am simply unable to keep up that seclusion which is so dear and so necessary to me.' More students were taking his classes; he had more than 120 enrolments for 'The Ethics of Christianity', although it was an advanced class and carried no credit, and he had the commitment of the Philosophical Club. Also, over and above his teaching, he continued to get requests to give public lectures. At such a public lecture at the Princeton Theological Seminary, its president and, it appeared to Bowman from the numbers present, most of the faculty turned out to hear him.

The department, though, was 'going to the dogs', Bowman told Kemp Smith. Fite was still chairman and relationships became more strained. There had been 'a dreadful slump in enrolments.' Overall student numbers taking philosophy were down by 50 per cent, with Bowman's classes being the exception.

It was against this background that Hibben again asked him if he would take over chairmanship of the department. This time Bowman accepted, but he said nothing about applying for a vacancy that would be coming up at Glasgow University: 'I hardly know how to approach Hibben on the subject. He'll certainly be very reluctant to let me even think of deserting this madhouse of a department, but that won't deter me.'

The department accepted Bowman as chairman and went along with the changes he introduced, but he had no illusions that it would last. Each member of the department seemed to pose problems and had to be handled differently: 'each member is a little vortex of anxiety for me. Scylla and Charybdis aren't in it.'

Managing the department took up time, but invitations to give lectures kept 'pouring in' on him. He turned down a request to give five lectures to 200 ministers over the summer, and the Princeton mission in Peking wanted him to come out for a year.

When the time came, Bowman sent in his application to Glasgow University for the chair of Moral Philosophy 'with no high hopes.' It was then that he told Hibben. He had expected the president to be annoyed, but he had no idea how upset he would be: 'He assured me that if I go it'll wreck the department.' However, Bowman pointed out that an application did not amount to much and told him that Kemp Smith felt it unlikely that he would succeed, but Hibben had the feeling that Bowman could not possibly be rejected.

In the event, however, he was unsuccessful but some of the University Court voted for him and he got positive feedback. Content with that, he immersed himself in work.

In the early days, although he had a modest view of his poetic powers, he kept a lookout for any review of *Sonnets from a Prison Camp*. It had been referred to in the *Glasgow Herald* but not, as far as he knew, in the States. Occasionally a student would produce a copy at the end of a class and ask for an autograph, and some colleagues commented favourably on his achievement and the originality of where he found his muse, but Bowman kept no note of any journal reviews. A year later, though, Bowman flagged up a meeting he had with a reader who was a real aficionado of his sonnets: he was an elderly banker from Baltimore, and Bowman does a neat send-up of the feedback and his own reaction:

> He had a copy given him as a present, and was overflowing with appreciation. I was a bit embarrassed. It's nice to be appreciated, but it's difficult to know what to say when the appreciation takes an American form. This old gentleman (so he says) sleeps with the Sonnets at his bedside, and takes them on railway journeys, and has been scattering them over the continent from Texas to New England! It rather gave me the feeling that they belonged to the same category as some well-advertised laxative which one should never be without and which one should recommend to one's friends.

However, family life was the important thing and it ran its course sweetly. Mabel became pregnant again and on 6 April 1923 gave birth to a boy. They called him Alastair.

That summer they were in Guysborough again for the summer vacation. For Archie it was bliss. He was well into a book he had been writing and outlined to Norman Kemp Smith the stage he had reached:

> I was progressing rapidly, and have nearly completed seven chapters, I wrote with a flowing pen and a degree of ease that surprised me. One reason, I think, is that I decided to write in the style that is natural to me, and not to try for a compression which I greatly admire (nowhere more than in your work) but which seems to be beyond my power. The result is a somewhat diffuse book, which I would willingly see reduced, if I knew how to reduce it without destroying it altogether.

That fall, two of Archie's brothers emigrated to America: on 14 September Alex and his wife sailed from Glasgow to New York, and two weeks later Jim and his wife and their little daughter set off. To begin with, they made Princeton their base, staying with Mabel and Archie until the brothers found work.

At the end of October Mabel's parents became very ill, and that implied responsibility that often falls on a daughter to care not only for her own children but also her elderly parents fell to Mabel. So, in early November 1923, Mabel took Maisie and the 6-month-old baby to Glasgow for what was to be the longest parting from Archie since the last year of the war.

However, they did not disrupt 8-year-old Ian's schooling and so he remained at home. With no distractions from a younger sister and a baby, Bowman decided it would be a good time to introduce Ian to classical Greek. This was the idea he had had when he was stationed at the permit office in Cologne: the whole family, he had imagined, could learn Greek together. However, Bowman was not trained in early child development and he found his formal methods of teaching an inflected language to a young child who had no conception of the parts of speech too challenging, but he decided that the important thing was to spend time together, father and son.

A few days after Mabel left, with Ian in the care of his aunts and uncles, Bowman was on his way to Washington and the White House with a delegation of academics who were to be introduced to the president of the United States. America, by this time, had taken an isolationist position; it had closed off immigration from several countries. Bowman was not there, though, in any lobbying capacity with his views on the world, and he gave himself up to the experience. He was very much taken with Washington: 'The beauty and grandeur of the city simply swept me off my feet. Washington is simply a dream.' However, he thought President Calvin Coolidge was a bit of a wet fish. The president shook hands with each of them, but 'hurried you through it. He is quite devoid of personal graces, but makes an impression of business-like despatch, which is not unpleasing.'

If the tight-lipped Calvin Coolidge gave nothing away of his thinking on points of national or international interest, there was a complete contrast for Bowman a few weeks later back at Princeton when he heard an address from a former student who was American vice-consul in Berlin, and he described it in a letter to Kemp Smith. It was in line with the analysis he had given him of German industrial power when he had been in the permit office in Cologne:

> I heard a really magnificent address on the German situation – by far the best thing I've listened to on the subject. It was given by Pen Davis [Nathaniel Penniston Davis], a son of Prof. Davis of the Seminary. Young Davis may have been one of your students. I had him in the first year of the war. He has been American Vice-Consul in Berlin, and his wife imparted to me yesterday that he is to return as Consul. His view is that the German industrial group of which Stinnes [Hugo Stinnes, industrialist of great wealth and power] is the head have sufficient

resources to meet all the needs of the situation but that no government Germany is likely to have will be strong enough to gain control of these resources. In the coming winter the $10,000,000 for which Germany asks will really be necessary to avert wide-spread starvation, and the fact that Germany could without difficulty supply this sum does not alter the fact that her poor will be allowed to starve if foreign aid is not forthcoming. Whatever happens, Mr Davis thinks that there is not the remotest chance of a successful communist uprising or of a successful coup-d'état. The republican form of government has come to stay. Mr Davis does not believe that the degradation of the currency was deliberately contrived by the government as a means to evade reparation payment. It was due rather to a policy of drift and is a phenomenon of governmental weakness. The only solution is for the German Government to admit its bankruptcy and submit to a foreign receivership; and there will be no way out unless the allied powers will consent to cooperate in a spirit of goodwill with the bankrupt state. Above all Mr Davis emphasised the absolute necessity of abandoning all hope of reparations for a period of years. That the resources are actually there makes an attitude and policy psychologically difficult; but the fact remains that there is no machinery known to man which can extort from the holders of wealth what they have decided not to place at the disposal of their country even in its hour of greatest agony. If this analysis is correct, it is a tremendous indictment of the industrial group, but, as Mr Davis pointed out, the same kind of thing goes on among other peoples, and I suspect he is not far wrong in this. One thing is fairly clear in my mind. It is quite useless to conduct human affairs along the lines of a rigid quid pro quo justice.

Still, that had been a rare opportunity for him to get insights into policy-level thinking about post-war Germany. The demands on his time came from nearer home, and they kept building up. 'The pressures on me to do this kind of thing are passing all bounds.' The most recent request came from President Hibben who roped him in to deliver a series of school lectures in New York.

The Spence School was a girls' independent school founded in 1892 by Clara B. Spence, who was also its first head. The school motto was (and still is): 'Not for school but for life we learn.' Clara B. Spence was thought by some to be ahead of her time as an educationist; she invited speakers of the calibre of Edith Wharton to give talks to the girls. Bowman had not heard of the school before, but friends at Princeton had. He wrote to Mabel: 'apparently Miss Spence's school is generally considered <u>the</u> élite school of New York. Mrs Atwood told me that nobody is the <u>thing</u> unless they have been to it.'

Bowman took the train to New York's magnificent Pennsylvania Station, and then walked to the school on W. 55th Street. In 1923, Miss McElroy had taken over as head from its founder and she told Bowman that the purpose of the lectures was 'to teach the girls common sense and prevent them giving way to the frivolities to which New York offers so many temptations.' The class was the seniors, a group of about fifty girls aged between 17 and 20. He formed a favourable impression of the school and he felt his first lecture had gone across well.

Over the next three months he continued with the course he had prepared and then he set an exam for the class. He marked the exam scripts and travelled up by train and, as usual, he sat in Pennsylvania Station finalizing his notes for the morning's lesson: 'I do enjoy those little sessions in the station. It is so tranquil there, and so bright. In some ways it's America at its best.'

He went to the school a little early as he wanted to discuss the exam papers with Miss McElroy. 'Miss McElroy is a nice person – rather elderly – and very calm and collected in her manner.' They went over the papers together and compared Bowman's grading of his exam results with the general assessment of the girls' class work and found, with about two exceptions, that they agreed. 'Miss McElroy was pleased at my trying to get reasoned answers rather than mechanical repetitions. So I think we are on a pretty good footing of understanding.'

The class was agog with excitement about the feedback. Bowman selected some of the answers and criticized them, then read out the best two papers as models. 'They were surprisingly good.' The best paper was by a girl who came up to speak to him with two others at the end of the lesson, 'and I soon saw how deeply the subject had taken hold of her. She is quite stirred up – at least as nearly so as such a lady-like person could be, and told me she is spending hours and hours thinking things over.'

Two weeks later, he himself acknowledged having thoughts that lay too deep to be expressed in words. Mabel wrote and told him that her father had died. She was a child, grieving the death of a parent, and Archie was wrenched that he could not be with her to comfort her.

He reminisced about past times, such as his asking her father for her hand in marriage. It happened on an afternoon outing to Kilfinnan where Mr and Mrs Stewart had taken Mabel and her boyfriend Archie:

> I had a hard job finding him and we were both a trifle shy about it, and very few words were spoken; but they were spoken heartily, and then, glad to make my escape, I hurried back to search for you, and found you and your mother on the bank of the Kilfinnan burn that your father fished so often. Do you remember it Beloved?

Then he went on to what he felt difficult to talk about:

> I have had such strange experiences of the spirit since you left and you were in the midst of them. I have not told you to trust in God. Somehow I find it difficult to speak about God, but what a reality He is to me. I trust absolutely in Him; and when we are together again I wish we could in some way find expression for our common sense of Him.

For all his outside commitments, though, Bowman had not become an absentee chairman of the Philosophy Department. He was determined to set up a new system of undergraduate study and he got it through, but there was hostility to it in the faculty. Bowman felt it was 'an almost incalculable advance for our academic ideas.' Students had to sit two papers of 4 hours each and one of 3 hours, making a total of 11 hours. During the exam the whole department was mobilized from 9.00 am to 11.00 pm. That triggered a new series of crises in the department that he had to sort out, but 'this sort of thing is sheer waste of life.'

Then came the shock of the unexpected from a distance of 5,000 miles. The chair of Moral Philosophy at Glasgow University fell vacant again, only two years after Bowman's unsuccessful application. The man who had been successful then, Alexander Lindsay, had now been appointed Master at Balliol College, Oxford. Although they were separated by an ocean, it seemed to Mabel and Archie that they were back on the same merry-go-round again: to apply or not to apply. This time, their decision was negative, and Bowman told Kemp Smith why:

> The only thing that would have induced me to repeat my application would have been my wife's desire that I should do so. When the chair fell vacant again I suddenly realized that it would be simply heart-breaking to leave Princeton, and when Mabel's cabled advice as to applying assumed the laconic form 'don't', it came with a sense of profound relief. At the same time I don't regard my present position as ideal. The question of nationality troubles me deeply. The idea of naturalizing is still almost unthinkable; yet to spend one's life an unenfranchised man is very painful. My roots are also still in the old country.

Although his roots were in Scotland, he was becoming familiar with America. He was scheduled, in the summer, to give a series of lectures at the University of California in Los Angeles.

By 1924, Hollywood was the world's leading film-making centre: the large studios were now dominant and Los Angeles became a sprawling magnet, attracting skilled artists and artisans from other film cultures across the globe. Bowman's reaction to it all was curious: 'My classes are small but very promising. The whole place, however, is disconcertingly feminine. To judge from first impressions, this is a city (and a university) of super-women. I am sedulously trying to avoid making acquaintances, so that the book may not be delayed.'

The book he was writing was for the Bross Foundation Prize. Towards the end of the nineteenth century, William Bross, a publisher and politician, had set up a foundation; money had been invested and every few years the foundation offered a prize of considerable worth for a book that dealt with the relationship between the findings in any field of knowledge and the Christian religion. Now Bowman had had a philosophical work on the go for the past four years. At first, as he gathered material for it, he had the provisional title *Naturalism and the Supernatural* in mind. Then he changed its direction. Kemp Smith kept urging him to get it finished and published. However, with his public lecture commitments and his chairmanship of the department, he let it drift: the price of his teaching and public engagements. Then, however, the secretary of the Bross Foundation wrote inviting him to submit a manuscript for the Bross Prize. In addition to the $6,000 prize, the Bross Foundation would publish the book. This was the goad he needed.

***

Mabel had been in Glasgow since November, and in that time her mother had become less capable of living on her own. If Archie had applied for and been appointed to the chair of Moral Philosophy when it came up the second time, Mable wrote: 'my problem about Mother will be solved for me.' She was left with the problem: none of her brothers were willing or able to help, Johnnie had no household other than the Stewart family home, Norman and his wife lived in Montreal, and Ronald and his wife 'seem reluctant to have their household upset in any way.'

Mabel could tell from his letters that Archie was feeling the strain of the long separation: he was missing her and the children, and he was overworking. He kept sending her bank drafts with money he received from his outside lectures and she was concerned about him. 'I feel more than ever convinced that I'd better come home in the autumn', and she would insist that Ronald and his wife take the mother until some other arrangement could be made. This was the plan they followed and, at last, in October Mabel returned to Princeton.

***

They were reunited as a family and family life resumed its even tenor, but only for a few months.

In March 1925, Kemp Smith wrote to Archie to tell him that their old former colleague Professor Latta, who held the chair of Logic and Rhetoric at Glasgow University, was letting it be known to his colleagues that he would have to retire on grounds of ill health. It would be the third time in as many years that a post would come up at Glasgow to which Archie was drawn.

In the meantime, his hopes for the Bross Foundation Prize had been dashed. The secretary of the foundation wrote informing him that someone else had won the prize. Bowman himself, after he sent the manuscript in, had felt that it required more work if it was to be published.

Then came a bolt from the blue ('the greatest honour I have ever had'): Sir Donald MacAlister, principal of the University of Glasgow, wrote to him: 'Would you allow me to bring forward your name as his [Professor Latta's] successor, and propose you to the Court for appointment?' The decision would be in the hands of the University Court, 'but I know that many of its members would gladly welcome you back to your old university.' He went on to outline the conditions: the salary would be £1,200 a year, together with a free house in the college quadrangle. Sir Donald asked for a reply before the court next met on 2 July.

Archie and Mabel were faced with the same dilemma that had confronted them twice before. In monetary terms there was nothing in it; the salary at Glasgow was about the equivalent of the $6,000 at Princeton. Mabel and Archie agonized over it, and decided it was to be Glasgow. So he went to Prospect and told President Hibben of 'the call' from Glasgow and that he intended to accept it.

Immediately, Hibben offered to raise his salary from $6,000 a year to $7,000 'on the spot – the matter being officially arranged the next day.' Then Hibben told him of a gigantic endowment campaign for the university – said to be about $20 million with moneyed interests like the Rockefeller Foundation behind it – that would lead to some departments, like Philosophy, being strengthened.

After going over it all again, Mabel and Archie reaffirmed their wish to move back to the old country, and Bowman cabled his acceptance to Sir Donald, on the condition that he remain at Princeton until February to clear up the department. He also wrote to Hibben, who was on the point of leaving on holiday.

By the next day word had leaked out and he began receiving telegrams begging him to remain in North America. 'All the time Mabel and I have been suffering almost unendurable anguish of mind. The desperately earnest appeal of Princeton not to desert her had penetrated too deep even for my resolution.'

In the afternoon, they went for a drive and returned to a telegram from the president of Hartford Theological Seminary, Connecticut 'imploring me in the name of the Seminary to stay in the interests of an Idealistic philosophy in this country. This was the last straw.' Mabel drove him to Prospect and he told Hibben that he would cancel his previous decision: he would stay at Princeton. 'Hibben's gratitude was most touching. He at once promised me a strong man to help bear the burden I have borne so many years. I mean, he has invited me to strengthen the department by selecting the best man I can find as a colleague.'

Then he cabled the principal of Glasgow University, cancelling his acceptance, and immediately after wrote to Kemp Smith: 'This is the most difficult letter I have ever had to write you, but I know you will understand and sympathise even if you do not approve.' He detailed all the moves up to that point of their deciding to remain at Princeton and 'that is the end of the story.'

However, it was not to be the end of the story. Mabel and Archie could not cut themselves off from the old country. Neither was it the end of the story because Glasgow University wanted him and there were some on the university court, like McNeile Dixon, who knew that Bowman must have had to go through much soul-searching to go back on his earlier decision.

The upshot was the principal of Glasgow University sending Bowman another cable: 'Wait February please reconsider', and Archie and Mabel did just that.

Because he did not have to take up the appointment until the next year, Bowman had time to see through the work of the session and make the department ready for the changeover.

On vacation in Quebec amid the Laurentian hills that summer, Bowman's thoughts were about the country he would be going home to in a few months. It had changed since the war; he thought that its time as a great power was on the wane. He expressed his thoughts about it to Kemp Smith on 20 August:

> Often I wonder whether our day as a first-rate power is passing… I think, too, that our tenure of political and commercial power in India and China (on which our financial prosperity so largely rests) will have to be largely modified. We can no longer go on doing things as we have been doing. A letter from my friend, Mr Wannamaker, Executive Secretary to our Peking work, gave some little revealing touches – not much in themselves but symptomatic of rottenness. Mr Wannamaker is on a visit to China and Japan. He says that the Chinese are taxed (by us) for the upkeep of public parks and bands. They are not permitted to enter the parks and if they want to listen to the music which their money maintains, they must pay while Europeans go free! On a previous visit to Shanghai he saw the announcement at the gates of the public park: 'Dogs and Chinese not admitted'. Of course that's not the whole of the picture, but it's evidence of much ugliness.

America, on the other hand, was developing, and since he first arrived in America in 1912 he had seen the enormous changes that were taking place in the country in the early part of the twentieth century. He gave his assessment of the way America was moving in a letter in the fall of 1925 to an educationist in the old country:

> The America of today is one of the most amazing phenomena of history, and the truth about it is very little known at home. So few Britons remain long enough to shed the veil of prejudice that prevents their seeing things as they are. It is not generally recognised that the American of today is above all categorised by modesty of demeanour, poise and slow deliberation, and that on the basis of these great qualities he is rapidly building up the greatest civilisation in the world. The advance of an authentic culture, as fine as anything the old world can show, is phenomenal. As an educationalist you would be thunderstruck by the universities. The resources behind them are fabulous. No university pays much attention to the benefactions that fall short of millions, and in the matter of material equipment and splendour they are getting far ahead of us. Their libraries and laboratories are magnificent. But what is more important, the faculties are fully alive to the fact that it is not in these things that true greatness lies, and the best places – Harvard and Princeton in particular – have achieved an extraordinary educational reform, which within a couple of years or so has rendered all the old standards obsolete. The attractions of life and work here are almost irresistible, and I had great difficulty in making up my mind to relinquish the unprecedented opportunities America offers.

As the months passed and the end of the year approached, he gave thought to a likely successor. The chairmanship of the department might well be filled by an insider, but who should be considered as the next holder of the Stuart Chair of Logic? He had already sounded out Kemp Smith, who said to him that he thought hardly any American philosopher would agree to a theistic philosophy, and that remark troubled President Hibben: it 'sticks in Hibben's throat.'

As to the choice he had made for his own future, he told Kemp Smith, he was now at ease about it:

> The passage of the months has confirmed me more and more in the rightness of the decision I made with such effort; and while the transition will be fraught with much pain, I don't think there will be any regrets to wrestle with. The regrets were all worked off in the painful weeks when I was summing up all the things that I should miss. As a matter of fact in many ways I'll be glad to leave America. With all its exuberant life, I

miss something essential, something I hope to find at home. – You think I take an unduly pessimistic view of the old country. I sincerely hope it may be so. But in America it's almost impossible to avoid such a view. The contrast between the situation here and at home is so startling.

Archie Bowman's last public address at Princeton was reported in the *New York Times*. He was described as 'one of the most popular lecturers at Princeton.' The talk was the last in a series on religion that had been arranged by the Princeton Philadelphian Society. Bowman's topic that evening was 'Religion and Life' and his emphasis, according to the newspaper, was that a unified personality was the basic gift that religion gives to life.

What Bowman deemed as something essential, he was to find in the old country.

Chapter Seven

Standard-Bearer

The war was the price this generation has had to pay for centuries of folly and centuries of wickedness. Paid in advance. Question is: what are we going to get?

Archie Bowman

That Saturday evening of 2 June 1928, Plato's star rose over Glasgow University as Bowman was talking to his audience about the qualities they should be looking for in the candidates they voted for at parliamentary elections, the men and women who sought high office, the people who would have the power to take the country into war.

It was an unusual gathering in the university's John McIntyre building: mainly cloth-capped shipyard workers, steel workers, miners, shop workers and the unemployed. They had turned out to hear Bowman give a talk, and there was nothing patronizing or gimmicky about it.

Here, in the old country, he found that 'something essential' which he could not have done in the United States as it stood on the sidelines of world events, out of the League of Nations. He had known broadly what he was looking for, and before he left Princeton he wrote to his old headmaster from schooldays in Ayrshire: 'I have always felt that a man should live and work, where possible, in his own country – and that most of all when things are not over-bright and the life of the nation is troubled by unrest and threatened by all sorts of disintegrating forces within and without.'

Bowman followed up on those ideas, and in the years that were left to him he served the cause of peace and championed the ideal of the League of Nations as the vehicle for bringing it about. That meant opening minds, promoting lifelong learning and empowering Everyman.

We have no notes from the lectures he gave in the prison camps: Bishop Arthur Karney said that he gave them without books and without notes, but Bowman wrote up full notes for the WEA meeting at Glasgow University and, as he warmed to his themes, they give a glimmering of the inner fire he found when he was lecturing hundreds of men in Rastatt and Hesepe prison camps.

He began his talk with the context of their working lives, and he shaped it towards the qualities they should be looking for in the nation's leaders.

Most of his audience would have had only the bare minimum of schooling required by law, but he started off on a positive note: 'We have come to realise that education is a process which is not confined to the early years of life. It begins with the first breath we draw; it goes on to the last.'

He alluded to it being a Glasgow University professor, Adam Smith, who invented the science of political economy and formulated the principle of free trade, 'a principle upon which, whatever its theoretical merits, our industrial prosperity in the nineteenth century was based, and which, in spite of numberless reverses in recent time, we still refuse to repudiate.'

The industrial system that developed from those principles created wealth for some but reduced 'working life to the monotony of machine-minding.' That same system, though, produced fast transport, mass printing and now, most recently, radio. As a result, he said, the worker

> can have his revenge upon the system that seemed to crush him by learning to master its workings in the light of a vast store of information placed nightly at his disposal. He will soon perceive that the moving forces in the world today are to be found not only in the outer realm of events, but in the inner world of thought, and will be driven to explore this realm in the books to which its secrets have been committed. In history, in literature, in science he will find a challenge to all the powers that are in him, and if he has character enough, will accept the challenge joyfully and resolutely.

However, that by itself was not enough. Bowman told his audience that a structure had been put in place to provide opportunities for learning, a structure with the universities working together with the education authorities. A driving force behind it was Sir Donald MacAlister, principal of the university. It meant that the university was no longer for the privileged few but a national institution: 'the framework has been provided. It's up to you, the members of the Workers' Educational Association, that we must look to for results.'

> Now what are these results to be? What is it in your power to do? In the first place you must adopt a more active – I might almost say a more aggressive attitude – to your own studies. It is not enough to sit in the classroom and listen to another man speaking. You must learn to speak for yourselves. You must become producers. You must add to your labours the pleasant labour of written exercises. Until you can bring your minds to bear upon your problems in this way you will not be in a position to reap the benefits of adult education. That these things are well within your powers I have no doubt whatever. I have had samples of your quality.

Two years ago I had the privilege of attending the annual meeting at which the representatives of the various classes report upon the session's work. On that occasion I listened to one of the finest speakers I have ever heard – a speech beautifully organised and executed, delicately humoured, mastered by high literacy distinction and concocted in Pollokshaws. It was a revelation of what you can do if you will only take the trouble to do it. The greatest obstacle to initiative and productivity is of course your natural modesty. But there is a way of getting round this obstacle. Where the individual suffers from unnecessary diffidence, he may feel confidence in the group. I would suggest that in every class after the first hour of formal instruction, you divide up into small parties for the purpose of discussion and perhaps for the production of written tasks. Of course it would greatly add to the effectiveness of the plan, if the groups in question were groups of friends. And if you cannot find congenial spirits with whom to work I would further suggest that you go out and bring them in. The recruitment of the Association is service for which we must rely almost entirely upon your efforts. If you are in earnest, if you feel that there is something to be gained from labours such as these, you should try to induce others to share the benefits with you. Each of you should be a missionary for the cause of adult education. I know that some of you are fully alive to your responsibilities in this respect. On the occasion to which I have just referred to, I had the further pleasure of listening to a member of the Association, a miner from Garngad (to whom, if he is present today I wish to pay my tribute of respect) describe how he scoured the country on his bicycle in the endeavour to secure recruits for the class of political economy. Such men are the salt of the earth, and a living witness to the truth that the old Scottish fervour for education is not dead within us.

You all have your circle of comrades and acquaintances, bench-mates and fellow workers. Above all you are in touch with a circle of the younger people. Nothing could be of greater importance than to enlist the interest of these. If adult education is to develop into the great thing we would like to see it, it must be linked up with the work of the schools and with the continuation classes… Continuity is the very essence of effective education.

However, Bowman then went on to warn about the downside of mass-circulation papers: the nation could be force-fed views, opinions and even falsehood at the behest of the owners. Here, he had a grievance of his own to air. In his two years back in the UK he had become considered newsworthy, not just in Scotland but by the national dailies. A few months earlier, the Educational Institute of Scotland (the EIS), the largest teachers' organization in Scotland, had invited him to give a talk at its annual congress at Ayr. His talk was entitled 'Human Nature and Education' but the press report of his talk was an embarrassment to him: it was framed as though he had given an anti-American address. He alerted Kemp Smith to it, for the latter was about to embark on a lecturing tour in the United States and had written to him for suggestions about New York hotels because Bowman's knowledge was more up-to-date than his. Bowman gave him the information he was looking for, and then went on:

> If by any chance you saw a newspaper report of a speech of mine in Ayr, in which certain criticisms of America appeared, I hope you will make allowances for the disconcerting ways of reporters. It is true, I used America as an illustration of certain tendencies which I was criticising in ourselves. But the thing was done in a jocular way and was quite incidental.

This was indeed the case. The EIS published his talk in its journal the following month. Bowman brought in references to the United States only in the last few paragraphs: American speech idioms – 'In America a place is not a place, but a location and if you wish to settle in it, you locate. If you travel daily to your business, you do not really travel, but you commute' – and he observed the tendency for these speech patterns to cross the Atlantic (a tendency that has continued ever since). In addressing an audience of schoolteachers, he could have assumed that, whatever their subject, they held to an implicit policy of correctness across the curriculum when it came to the spoken word.

He told Kemp Smith that the newspaper report 'omitted all that was most serious and gave a most erroneous impression of my speech as a whole. There were also errors. I said: "The Americans are not an idle people", which appeared as "the Americans are not an _ideal_ people."'

So that June evening, speaking to the WEA, Bowman brought up the topic with feeling. He cited a company, Aberdeen Newspapers Ltd, which was the target of a hostile takeover bid by the parent company of one of the large national papers. Aberdeen Newspapers produced the *Aberdeen Press and Journal*, a fusion of two earlier papers, the *Evening Gazette* and the *Free Press*, and it professed no political allegiance, giving coverage to all political parties. Bowman brought up the subject this way:

> A mentally apathetic people is a source of weakness to the country. Such a people is unable to assert itself where self-assertion is most necessary, and it falls a ready victim to every prowling predatory power. It has no

mind and no will of its own. It takes the opinions, the literature, the music, the pictures that are thrust upon it, and it does not know how to defend itself and to protest. Under such conditions freedom, in the sense that freedom is a state of the soul, becomes a sham and a delusion; and we in Scotland are in deadly danger of losing our freedom and our national independence. You must have noticed from the newspapers that the people of Aberdeen are about to lose their free press. The newspaper magnates of the south – those robber-barons of the twentieth century – are fighting over their prostrate form. Henceforth presumably they will take their political opinions at the hand of an absentee dictator. To such a level has Scotland sunk.

Finally, he turned to leadership, and he had an ideal for the sort of person who should fill the roles of leadership at state level. When he had been in Hesepe prison camp, he recalled his student days and he wrote that he had 'laboured long in labouring seas / Pledging my soul to martyred Socrates; / And o'er night's face the star of Plato rose.' On that evening of his talk to the WEA in Glasgow University Union, Plato's star rose again.

Plato had argued that there will be no end to the troubles of states, or indeed of humanity itself, till philosophers become kings in this world, or till those we now call kings and rulers really and truly become philosophers, and political power and philosophy thus come into the same hands. Bowman did not use the word philosophers, but expressed the idea in terms of men and women who have a rich life of the mind that imbues their practical savvy:

> This state of affairs would not be so bad if those who have assumed the dictatorial role, the leaders of public thought and public life, were in all cases worthy of the national trust – if they were men to whom the public could look up to with that confidence and reverence which are due to true leadership. But in the present age such men are rarely to be found in the highest offices of state. If you have been reading Lord Oxford's memories, as these have been appearing from day to day in the *Glasgow Herald*, you will have suffered a sense of disappointment and disillusion. The history of the cabinet during these war years is not an edifying story. The personages presented to us were not impressive personages. It is difficult to feel that the highest interests of the nation were safe in their hands. And yet they were the nation's choice. They represented with considerable accuracy the minds of the people who put them where they are. It is not that they are bad men, but merely that they are superficial. What one feels about them is that their minds have never been trained

to take a deeply serious, a deeply-understanding view of life, and the poorness of their mental quality is reflected in their conduct of affairs. There are still among us I am glad to say, survivors of a finer breed – some of them in office. I can think of one or two; and you can also. Now when you consider these men, you will observe that while they differ in their views and their political affiliations, there is one thing they have in common. They are all men of books as well as men of affairs... They all have an inner as well as an outer life; and the latter is the externalisation of the former. That is the secret of their dignity, their probity, their mellow wisdom. That such men should be forthcoming is a vital need of the nation; and it is no less necessary that we should know them when we see them, and that we should place them where they may serve us best. Whether or not we shall succeed in this depends upon our own discernment, and for discernment we need trained minds and the power of judgment. It is to cultivate these qualities within us that the WEA has been called into existence... The future of our country is in the hands of the people. The future of the people depends upon their willingness to put forth the effort required to train themselves for that knowledge which is one with power.

Know them when we see them! Bowman said at one of his talks that Woodrow Wilson's leadership had been 'providential'; it was an example of political power and philosophy in the same hands, for it was the president of the United States, once Professor of Philosophy at Princeton, who was the national leader who promulgated 'Fourteen Points' for world peace, the document that became the basis for the Treaty of Versailles. His paper was instrumental in creating the League of Nations.

In Bowman's view, there was now a chance, after the Great War, when there was a breathing spell, to make peace secure:

'The coming of the League,' Bowman wrote in the *Scots Observer*, 'has changed all our perspectives and widened all our horizons. Before its advent these perspectives, these horizons, were limited by our own interests, our own national enterprises. We assumed no responsibility for the welfare of mankind, for the future of the world.'

So advocacy of the League of Nations became the main focus of his public commitments. He gave speeches up and down the country in church halls, town halls, the House of Commons and at meetings of League of Nations secretaries; he also wrote articles for newspapers and journals.

Bowman had not turned pacifist though. He held more or less to the old definition of the 'Just War'. He put it as follows:

> If the cause is unambiguously righteous (and who can ever be sure of this?) it does not cease to be so because it must be maintained by force. And if we are constrained to believe that there is no other way, if every attempt at a peaceable solution has been tried and found wanting, then the righteousness of the cause sanctifies the war that is fought on its behalf. In this case, the course of the Christian is clear. He should be the first in the field.

He put a lot of work into his talks, framing them in terms of the audience he would be addressing and the international situation of the moment. In the late 1920s, the means of achieving a safer world, Bowman told his audience, was through Cosmopolitanism and Internationalism. He accepted that there was a tension between the nation and the League but, as he saw it, the League did not displace old loyalties and the national spirit was too precious to be destroyed. He saw it as the League enabling 'the state to work in the larger service of humanity: "Britain for the world; Britain for humanity."'

In the years up until 1930, he could point up the successes of the League in defusing international disputes; disputes that might not have received press coverage in the UK: resolving a dispute between Sweden and Finland over possession of the Åland Islands; and when Greece made armed incursions into Bulgaria, Bulgaria's appeal to the League resulted in Greece withdrawing.

However, by 1930 the tone that comes through in his public speeches is one of frustration at this country's leaders dragging their feet when it came to disarmament. At local public meetings, he tended to have hand-written notes in the form of headings on which he enlarged from the platform:

I
No longer a question on whether we shall have a League.
The only question: what shall we do with it?

II
No longer at liberty to do anything we like
Active policy of peace and disarmament.
No longer a question whether we shall disarm
We are irrevocably pledged to do so.
We compelled Germany to disarm.
We have not yet done so ourselves.

By 23 March 1932, however, there was more than frustration when he addressed an annual meeting of secretaries of the League of Nations at the Ca' d'Oro building: Bowman excoriated the League for its failures. This speech was fully written up and very detailed in background, current situation and analysis of the shortcomings of member nations. His focus was on Japan's invasion of Manchuria, China's appeal to the League, and the League's lack of response:

> On surveying the course of events, our first impression is one of profound disappointment. It would hardly be too much to say that the League has tragically failed. It has in this instance proved itself powerless to prevent a great catastrophe and (what is worse) the very kind of catastrophe which it was specially designed to render impossible. We now realise that under the regime of the League the same kind of international disaster which we were accustomed to expect <u>before there was a League of Nations</u> is still possible. Indeed, <u>in a way</u>, what has happened has been worse than anything that could possibly have happened before 1920, because before 1920 any breach of faith between nations affected only the nations directly and indirectly concerned. But Japan's action in China involves not only a breach of international obligations in the ordinary sense of the term: it involves a breach of obligations that have about them a peculiar degree of sanctity and solemnity. Japan has broken faith not only with China, but with the League. That is to say she has foresworn her word of honour pledged to 54 sister nations and publically proclaimed to the whole world by her signature to the Covenant.

He went on to say that the existence of the League was at stake; it had not become effective 'in imposing the principles of international action upon the policies of a really powerful and headstrong nation.'

Then, on 8 December 1932, Bowman took his argument to the highest level, the House of Commons, where he gave an address to Glasgow members of parliament:

> I wish to draw the attention of Members to the fact that the youth of this country has become more and more restive under the repeated failure of the nations to live up to their obligations as signatories to the Covenant of the League.
>
> The attitude of the younger generation in particular, and more specifically of the educated youth of the universities, is one of growing exasperation. In proof of this may be mentioned the recent manifesto on Disarmament by young Oxford dons, and the indignation meeting held last Spring at

Glasgow University on the initiative of all three political parties acting in conjunction. The purpose of this meeting was to protest against the inactivity of the Government in view of the Sino-Japanese situation.

Since then the attention of the public has been chiefly focused on the Disarmament question. The point has been reached at which another failure would so impair the prestige of the League of Nations as to render its survival problematic. That is a contingency which would be too terrible to contemplate. Its effects upon every one of the nations involved would be tantamount to that of a crushing defeat in war. To avert such a disaster is a responsibility which devolves upon the statesmen of the nations concerned, and in the case of Great Britain the whole power of Parliamentary Government must be brought into action to secure the end desired. Disarmament is not optional. The nations within the League are pledged to it. The only questions which remain open are those which are to do with the time, the rate and the extent of the operation, and these points can no longer be considered as altogether within the option of the nations. [He was referring to the opening sentence of Article 8 of the Covenant of the League of Nations.]

The members of the League recognise that the maintenance of peace requires the reduction of national armaments to the lowest point consistent with national safety and the enforcement by common action of international obligations.

However, whether there was any discussion around those points or whether the honourable members merely listened politely, Bowman does not say. Certainly the MPs had their own priorities and concerns in their constituencies, for these were the years of the Depression with millions unemployed.

The task of preventing widespread starvation was tackled at governmental level by paying out dole money, but the long-term unemployed needed more than a subsistence-level life if they were to keep their sense of self-worth and this need was not met by political action. So voluntary schemes grew up in parts of the country to create work for the unemployed and, as an extension of his work with the WEA, Bowman got involved.

As an ex-prisoner of war, he knew what it was like to find life lacking a sense of purpose: 'Around my cage's circuit I have paced / Sunk in myself, and broodingly have traced / These late appalling issues', and he travelled across the country visiting projects that were creating work for the unemployed or retraining them in new skills.

Then, at a series of public meetings, he elaborated on the projects, giving examples of what was being done – they could be replicated, or spark ideas for what could work in a different setting – for these were not large-scale schemes promoted by the altruistic wealthy, they were initiated by professional people such as clergymen, lecturers and artists.

Bowman called his talk 'Work with the Unemployed – an Opportunity for Service.' The line he took was to stress the spiritual needs of a person deprived of making a contribution to society: 'The self-respecting man who knows the worth of what he has to give, feels affronted and humiliated in a world that has no use for him.' From his experience of life in a prison camp, he knew the mindset that develops – listlessness and apathy – and if these are allowed to remain, he said, they lead to 'complete demoralisation.'

He would go on to give examples of what a group was doing. In one case, a minister of religion took the initiative, gathered together a management committee, and they got access to a derelict linen factory in Dunfermline, recruited unemployed to make the building watertight and installed work benches: 'the transformation was achieved by a group of miscellaneous workmen, who gave their services freely and without any thought of remuneration.' They were then able to produce useful household articles and traded them within the group; it was a principle that any goods produced could not be traded on the open market. One project was retraining fifty men to become cobblers. A local artist formed a painting workshop. Another scheme was set up by a university lecturer, who recruited unemployed: they got scrap material from the Clyde shipyards and made furniture which they sold within the group, the members paying up at 6d a week, but no article could be taken until it was paid for. Mutual service was the keynote of these ventures.

By now, though, Bowman had a very heavy workload, for his outside public commitments were not at the expense of his university work: he rewrote his lectures every two years, and when Hector Hetherington (who had been appointed to the chair of Moral Philosophy at the time Bowman did not apply), left Glasgow to become vice-chancellor of the University of Liverpool, Bowman was appointed to the chair, ceding that of Logic and Rhetoric. He completed a three-year appointment as dean of the Faculty of Arts (although he wriggled out of the expectation that the incumbent would automatically do a second stint).

He had a six-month respite in 1929 when he was given leave of absence from Glasgow University to lecture at the University of California at Berkeley. Bowman made a family holiday of the first few weeks; their first visit to America since they had left Princeton. In the early days in Glasgow, Maisie had some longing for Princeton, but she and her brothers took to life in the Square, the large quadrangle at the university where the principal and the professors and their families were housed. It was a community of academics and their children, and a great place for forming friendships. All three of them had piano lessons; Ian also played the bagpipes and Alastair the cello. Later on, it was in the Square that Ian learned to drive. All of them, though, had memories of Princeton and they were looking forward to those weeks of holiday.

It passed all too quickly, and then came the parting when Mabel and the children returned to the UK and Archie set off westward by road for California and the start of the academic year at Berkeley. As a couple, their love for one another had not dimmed with the years and a few days after he stopped over at Albany, Archie wrote to Mabel: 'My Own Beloved, I have not written you for quite a number of days, but I have been just terribly near you in spirit, and I have been loving you with an intensity of love that is almost pain.'

He enjoyed the months at Berkeley, but towards the end of his time there he was looking forward to being reunited with his family, and at the same time bracing himself for the workload that lay ahead. On 10 December, he wrote to Kemp Smith:

> My sojourn in Berkeley is drawing to a close, and in a few days I turn my face eastward. It has been a very profitable time for me and a blessed respite from the all-but-impossible conditions of life in Glasgow. I have enjoyed the blessing of seclusion, and have been able to accomplish a good deal both in reading and writing.

However, when he returned from Berkeley, he took up public commitments again with renewed vigour, yet he could have given them all up and accepted an attractive offer of a job he would have loved.

The crunch came in January 1930: Princeton wanted him back. He was offered a professorship, similar to that held by A.N. Whitehead at Harvard, at a salary of $9,000.

Bowman's response was puzzling: he sat on his hands and did not reply, but President Hibben had an administrative deadline (as Bowman well knew from his own experience). On 10 February Hibben asked R.B.C. Johnson, chairman of the Philosophy Department, to write to Bowman explaining that they had to have a decision by the beginning of March for the upcoming year's staffing and budget. That same day, Johnson wrote to Bowman asking him to cable his decision, but still Bowman did not respond.

Finally, near the end of June, he wrote to Johnson: 'I know well that you are both surprised and pained by my long silence, but I think you will understand the reason for it. There are some letters which it is almost impossible to write, and this is one of them.' He admitted: 'It never really came to a clear decision. I simply couldn't say "no" and I couldn't make my mind up to say "yes."' What had been on offer was so attractive: 'the life most dear to me – the life of scholarly retirement and philosophical preoccupation.' Yet he felt he had a duty to stay. He told Johnson the way he felt was like fifteen years earlier when he went to war: 'like Luther "I can do no other."' However, this time the call was to stay: 'here I can be of use.' Yet at the same time he acknowledged: 'Whether what I am doing amounts to anything is not for me to ask. My business is to go on doing it, and to take the rest on trust.'

So Bowman carried on with a heavier load of public meetings than ever, championing the League. The seriousness of changing events increased in the early 1930s and the tone of his speeches darkened, for history's jackboots were marking time. The month after he talked to members of parliament, Adolf Hitler was elected chancellor of Germany.

At a meeting in a small Lanarkshire town, Bowman began his talk by outlining the evil of modern warfare:

> Inversion of all moral standards:
> War turns every form of wickedness
> Into a military virtue.
> (1) Destroys chivalry. From very nature of the case
> denies the right to defend.
> Spares neither sex nor age.
> Brutal cowardice of modern war.
>
> (2) Substitutes anarchy for honour.
> Breaking promises a military necessity.
> Necessity <u>knows no laws</u>.

Then he went on to distinguish between the nation and the state: he defined the nation as 'the body of people living in the same country and sharing the same life.' The state he described as 'the body of people living under the same system of government.' He went on that it was the state that makes war, it is the nation that suffers, and it is 'the suffering of the nation (i.e. the people) that leads the state to sue for peace.'

> Now my idea is that the nation should not only compel the State <u>to sue for peace in time of need</u>, but should labour to induce the State <u>to keep the peace at all times</u>.
> This is the essence of Internationalism – to utilise all the kindliness and friendliness inherent in people with a view to improving inter-state relations.

However, he acknowledged that Internationalism implied a democratic system of government and said that there was a 'repudiation of Democracy at present day.' He also recognized that the League of Nations 'cannot operate in a world of Dictators.' However, he believed that it was only a matter of time until 'Democracy will come surging back.' That Britain had a role in this, he argued: 'We must show that Democracy is not only the finest system of government, but the most efficient. We must make it so – in the things that count.'

His next League speech was more high-profile: he spoke at a League of Nations Lunch at the Ca' d'Oro again and delivered an analysis of the present plight of the League: 'its condition was critical but not dead.' He elaborated that, for the moment, the key to the situation was held by Mussolini; he read out part of page 11 of the document attributed to Mussolini: 'The Political and Social Doctrine of Fascism.' He referred to other revolutions: France, the USA, Soviet Russia and more recently the situation in Italy and Germany. He felt that the new danger was of competing propagandas, those of communism and fascism; the world was divided for the first time on a principle.

Bowman put a lot of detail into his speeches, researching the background, analysing the changing world political climate. He in no way recycled old talks. By this time, he was probably the most widely-recognized and publicly-quoted figure in Scotland upholding the ideals of the League of Nations.

However, no one maintains such a high public profile for long without being sniped at from the ranks of his *confrères*, and it was said of Bowman that 'he had a low flash-point, with enthusiasms easily aroused.' Norman Kemp Smith, though, refuted that notion. He said that Bowman was fastidious in his choice on what to give himself up to, that he followed no fashion and took his own line.

This is backed up by Bowman's notes for his public activities and from the articles written by him. They cluster around a group of social concerns: foremost by far was promoting world peace, and next, empowering Everyman through education and retraining. Then as a theistic philosopher, he was invited to give talks to church organizations such as the General Assembly of the Church of Scotland, and he spoke at a summer school on Theology at St Andrews and occasionally at a meeting in a YMCA. Also he had long supported the temperance movement.

Also, as an Ayrshire man, a writer of verse and a lover of poetry, he would give 'The Immortal Memory' (a formal tribute to Robert Burns) at a Burns Supper. At one of these talks, he showed his contempt for the religious dogmatism that at one time had dominated life in Scotland.

In January 1931, he was invited to give 'The Immortal Memory' address at the Falkirk Burns Club, and he spoke of the bold stance 'the man o' independent mind' took against the church tyranny of his day. He placed Robert Burns in the context of the Enlightenment, and he described the Enlightenment as 'the resurgence of man's free spirit against a long-established tyranny, whether in church or state, in social usage, in artistic convention or in modes of thought. Its instruments are ridicule and reason.' Then he went on to outline the church tyranny brilliantly satirized by Burns:

> In the age of Burns our Scottish Calvinism, sealed in the hearts of the people by the blood of the martyrs had become a national incubus. Calvinism by itself, as it comes down to us from Augustinian sources, is a noble doctrine, the sum and substance of it is the belief the insistence – fundamental to all true religion – that to God and not to man should be the glory. Unfortunately our Scottish theologians were prone to think of God's glory chiefly in terms of man's damnation. Religion had become a one-sided transaction in which there was no role for the human subject, but one of fatalistic submission to the inscrutable decrees of Providence. Nothing that man could do by moral effort of his own could do or could become had any weight with the Divine disposer of his destiny. Our doom was sealed to us from all eternity, and the ways of God were not finding out. This was the view of religion which Burns received with withering scorn and with uproarious laughter in the greatest satire ever written.

At this point in his talk Bowman read aloud the first verse of Burns' poem, *Holy Willie's Prayer*, in which we overhear a Calvinist – one of the elect – at his devotions:

> O Thou, wha in the Heavens dost dwell,
> Wha, as it pleases best thysel',
> Sends ane to heaven and ten to hell,
> A' for thy glory,
> And no for ony guid or ill
> They've done afore thee!

Although that interpretation of Calvinism would subsequently be overturned by another theology, that of the 'New Lights', it was a long time coming and the old held on doggedly:

> There is no characteristic of the Scottish mind more typical than its dour tenacity; and the men of Burns' day were true to type. What they had won they were determined to hold; and their right to their creed, and their right to believe in hell, and to believe in it in their own way, was something they had won with the best blood of their hearts. To their hearts accordingly, they clasped and treasured thought. Sabbath day

by Sabbath day they crowded to the kirk to listen, terror-stricken yet entranced, to the recital of the tortures that awaited most of them; and the power to bring these tortures home to the imagination was what they most appreciated in a preacher. Reputations rested on this power. The English are said to take their pleasures sadly. 'Sadly' is not the word to describe the pleasure-taking of these theologically-minded eighteenth-century Scots. They could not enjoy themselves at all, they could not warm to it, until they felt the breath of hell fire on them.

Hence that titanic laughter in the soul of Robert Burns. But came it that he 'a simple country bardy', as he calls himself could perpetrate such impropriety? How had he of all men the heart to laugh in the presence of so many 'lang wry faces'? Why, sinner that he was, had the rigours of a Calvinistic theology no terrors for him? No doubt the emancipation began with some influence from that liberal-minded man, his father. No doubt something of the first stirrings of a more enlightened view among the cultivated classes and the clergy of the 'new light'. But it is to Burns himself and what is quintessential in him that we must look for the deeper explanation. In Burns the logic of the heart had overcome the logic of the pulpit: instinct had proved too much for dogma. Two great forces had met in the breast of a poet, an affronted moral reason and an outraged feeling for humanity. The result was an explosion and the thundercloud that had brooded over the spirit of Scotland lifted from the soul of Burns leaving two things in its place, a mind swept clean of superstition and a heart grown passionate with faith.

Bowman had no party-political affiliations. He gave what he said was his first political speech about six months before his death and he gave it, he said, 'as a non-party man.' It was in support of Sir Godfrey Collins, a candidate for the National Government, because 'elements from all parties can vote for him.' Collins had been Secretary of State for Scotland, and one of the decisions Bowman attributed to him was bringing the Scottish Office to Edinburgh.

He also wrote an article on Scottish identity that still has resonance. It appeared in a newspaper under the heading: 'When a Nation is not a State: The Problem for Scotland.' He wrote it in response to the Chief Scout, Lord Baden-Powell's 'refusal to permit the use of the balmoral [hat] to Scottish Scouts.' Yet the underlying issues Bowman explored have had continuing relevance.

Bowman's weakness was not that he rose to any lure that came his way; his weakness was his health and it always had been. He had suffered from colitis from boyhood into manhood, and his health became less and less equal to supporting the stress to which he subjected himself. In the army he had been graded B1, and that was on the strength of the MO not putting him through a medical (other than an eye test), relying, he said, on his past knowledge of Bowman. However, Bowman's comrades in the battalion (from the inference in his letters) doubted that he could withstand life in the trenches, and certainly Mabel had concerns that he would suffer from the effects of gassing more than most men.

He survived winter in the trenches though. Then came the watershed when he was a PoW and he discovered the extent of his gifts for teaching and communicating. He used his gifts to great effect at Princeton, and when he came back to Glasgow, he really drove himself with his public commitments, year after year, for underpinning it all was his conviction that he had to serve society and he did that according to his lights.

His academic standing remained high, and in May 1933 he was invited to Princeton to give the Vanuxem lectures in 1934. These were a series of public lectures founded in 1912. Bowman wrote to Kemp Smith: 'I am naturally pleased that they have thought me good enough to give the Vanuxem Lectures in Princeton, and it will be a real joy to visit the place where so many happy years were spent.'

He and Mabel would find changes since their time there. President Hibben had retired in 1932. He had been a great supporter of Bowman and only two months before the Vanuxem invitation arrived, both Hibben and his wife were killed in a car accident. They had one daughter, Beth Grier, whom Mabel knew well.

The invitation meant that Bowman would have to do a lot of preparatory work before and after the lectures. The lectures were to be published, and his instructions were that they should not be published in the form in which they were delivered. He told Kemp Smith: 'with a programme already for a year in advance, I shall have little enough time to write the book.'

When he was about halfway through his heavy schedule for the year, his health broke down and for a while it was feared he might have to pull out of the Vanuxem invitation. He rallied, though, and in February he wrote to R.B.C. Johnson at Princeton:

> Under the strain of the last seven years my health has given way, and is unlikely to be equal to my commitments for a long time to come. This will have to be my apology for many deficiencies. But out of evil, good. The doctor absolutely refuses to let me travel unless Mabel is there to look after me.

On 24 February 1934, Archie and Mabel sailed from Glasgow. That evening, Mabel wrote in her diary that the Firth of Clyde was bathed in beautiful winter sunshine, and that the Isle of Arran had a diadem of cloud.

They at length reached Princeton on 5 March. The Vanuxem lectures were a series of six, and the opening lecture was scheduled for Tuesday, 13 March. The series of lectures was held in No. 10 McCosh. Mabel went with him to the first of them. His opening tribute appeared in the Princeton Alumni Weekly, 6 April 1934.

Bowman rose to his feet and began:

> The thought that is uppermost in my mind at this moment is the thought that when I last spoke from this platform it was to say 'Good-bye' to Princeton; and the last word was uttered, not by me, but by one whom I had fondly hoped to greet today. Of President Hibben I cannot trust myself to speak. He was my friend. It was he who brought me here; and it is to him that I owe the ten happiest years of my life. For more than twice that period he presided over the destinies of this great University with wisdom, courage and devotion. His administration covered the dark days of the war and the mad race of the years that followed. But throughout the bewildering oscillations of that period he remained calm and steadfast at his post, resting his cause on a faith that never faltered or gave way. For such a life we are moved to profoundest gratitude; and if you will not consider it presumptuous on my part, I should like to think of these Vanuxem lectures as in some sense a belated and imperfect offering to the memory of a friend and a leader, and so to rest my tribute of love and reverence upon the spot where now he rests.

Later that evening, in her diary Mabel wrote: 'Large attendance and great enthusiasm. Paid beautiful tribute to late President Hibben, which greatly comforted Beth Grier.'

No. 10 McCosh was the room in which Bowman used to give a course of general lectures to graduates and the public, and at that first lecture he saw that 'there were many of the same faces in the audience.'

However, by 20 March, Mabel realized that Archie was exhausted. When the series of lectures was finished, they had time for touring around. Bowman was interested to see what effects the Depression was having in America. Although their impressions had to be superficial, they did not come across the evidence of deprivations that were a daily sight back home. Bowman was only once accosted by a beggar in the time he was in the country, and that was on the Princeton Campus. 'Perhaps the most startling sight we saw was that of the unemployed sleeping on the subway stairs in New York.'

With his involvement in voluntary schemes for the unemployed at home, Bowman was interested to see some of the results of President Roosevelt's New

Deal policy, which directed federal funding into a huge programme of public works. Despite the Depression having put the brakes on the American enterprising spirit for advancement, he discovered that astonishing advances had still been made in spite of it. In Washington, there had been 'an amazing programme of building.' He had always been impressed by what American buildings expressed about the power and enterprise of the country: some years earlier in an article he had described 'titanic structures, cubistic and pyramidal, which enshrine the spirit of commerce, office buildings that are temples and temples that are railway terminals.'

He and Mabel then went on to Philadelphia to see his brother, Jim, and found there too that the city had greatly advanced. From there they travelled to Montreal, where Bowman gave a lecture to medicals at McGill University. He told Kemp Smith about how their former colleague at Princeton, Charles Hendel, was doing. Hendel had gone from Princeton to McGill in 1929 to take up the chair of Moral Philosophy. Bowman told Kemp Smith: 'He is universally esteemed. In fact I was told he is the most respected of the Arts professors, and the students adore him.'

Looking back at the lectures in the McCosh, Bowman wrote Kemp Smith:

> we were rather overwhelmed by the experience and by the unbelievable warmth of our welcome. The people there have carried kindness to the point where it almost hurts. I look back upon the years at Princeton as the most idyllically happy period of my life, and I suffer from periodic and violent nostalgia for the place and the people.

Yet this was the life on which he had turned his back in 1930 when he had the option of returning to it.

At the beginning of October, Archie and Mabel returned to Glasgow and the family was reunited. Maisie began her first year of an arts degree, and Ian was now in the third year of his course. Bowman resumed his role with the same enthusiasm as before.

His brother, Alex, who was a doctor and who worked in a medical practice in Princeton, had been diagnosed with TB of the spine. He chose to go to Glasgow on his own for treatment as there was a doctor there whom he particularly trusted. After he had been treated he returned to Princeton but then, in 1935, he brought his family back to Glasgow and for a time they stayed with Mabel and Archie until he became established in a city practice.

At some point in the 1935/36 academic session, Archie's 'old enemy' attacked him again and so severely that his health broke down. He recovered but had to have a period of convalescence. Yet he was far from idle. On 23 May 1935, he wrote to Kemp Smith:

> In spite of the medical embargo on all outside activities I have found this a hard year – possibly because I have rewritten my class lectures and have worked up a new honours course on Kant's Third <u>Critique</u>. This work has militated against the completion of my book – on which, indeed, I have done no work at all for some time. I hope to finish it in the summer. I have also been plagued by an old familiar demon – the irresistible love of poetry, and I have written a volume of verse which I may publish later on – not at present, however, as I should not want to have it precede my Princeton Lectures.

Before the end of the year, Bowman was back in the public forum, this time speaking at the Glasgow branch of the League of Nations. He challenged the most recent peace proposals of the British and French governments and condemned what the two governments had proposed. According to *The Scotsman*, he said: 'Britain, to all appearances has definitely forsworn all the principles of the League.' He proposed and succeeded in having the Glasgow branch send a resolution to the prime minister and foreign secretary urging that the government continue with a policy of sanctions and 'to support no settlement of the Abyssinian dispute which failed to make it clear that aggression did not pay.'

Three months later, on 17 March 1936, Bowman gave a talk at the Freedom Club. He had done his research on Italy's vulnerability to oil sanctions. His topic was 'Sanctions and the League'. He reiterated the British position as stated in 1932: 'keep the coercive and mediatory functions of the League distinct.' He went on to give two examples of the vulnerability of the war machine to oil sanctions – a fighter plane using 50 gallons per hour; a tank or lorry 10 miles per gallon – and he reminded his audience that League countries supplied almost 90 per cent of Italy's oil: 'Rumania 34%; Russia 22; Iran 12; Dutch colonies 10; France 4.' In a wide-ranging account of where the League could have been proactive, he came to what he headed the moral significance of Hitler's recent actions:

(i) Reassertion of Freedom in German sense. Hitler as Liberationist.
(ii) Refusal to accept external tribunal. Germany to be sole judge of her actions. Will not recognise alien court of justice.
(iii) Impossibility of entering League on these terms or of accepting policy of sanctions.
(iv) Crucial point – Hitler's eastern policy – Russia.

Unfortunately his notes give no suggestion how he developed this point, but time was running out for Bowman.

The town of Beith, where he had been born fifty-three years earlier, was where he gave his last public speech. It was on Thursday, 23 April 1936. Mabel went along with him and she drove the car. The talk was held in the High Church hall. There was a large turn-out for a son of the town, and the local newspaper the *Beith Supplement and Advertiser* sent a reporter.

Bowman called his topic 'The World Situation and the Cause of Peace', and he aimed it at a more general level than his talk for the Freedom Club. He began by summarizing the failure of the League's position in relation to Japan's aggression against China, and he referred to political expediency in our own country. A few months earlier, in reply to a question raised in the House of Commons as to why the League had not supported China, the government spokesman Sir Samuel Hoare replied that it was because China never asked them. According to the local newspaper, Bowman emphasized that he did not wish to impugn the distinguished statesman, but the answer was hardly in accordance with the facts: 'The truth was that from the moment the situation began to develop, China kept issuing frantic appeals to the League of Nations to support her.'

Then Bowman turned to the more recent aggression with Mussolini's forces invading Abyssinia. He told his listeners that the League had power to impose sanctions, and he spoke about the confusion in the public mind about sanctions; they were not optional, they were definitely prescribed. He went on to say that it was strange to think that a century ago Italy was in the forefront of the struggle for liberation; today she was a nation in chains and she was dragging her chains with her into Abyssinia. About 90 per cent of Italy's oil was imported from League countries, yet oil sanctions against the country were not being applied. Also, according to the reporter, he made a point of stressing the amazingly paradoxical situation: the enemies of the League of Nations were to be found within the League itself.

Yet Bowman's was not a message of despair, of resignation to the political forces that move events on the grand scale. He referred to the power of public feeling that a few months back 'forced the government to abandon an agreement that would have meant shame and disgrace.' According to the newspaper report, he told his listeners: 'We must train our minds and consciences in political integrity; we must keep the flame of political interest alive, not in a narrow party spirit, but upon the ethical plane.' Individuals, he said, should raise their voices if their country was party 'to anything that was ethically disgraceful.' He also exhorted his audience that they must labour within the limit of their power, and there was one thing that all could really do: 'we could strive to make a reality of these ideals of freedom and peace which we would like to see established on an international scale in our individual life.'

He finished his talk with a vision of a renewed League that would again emerge from the cloud 'which presently obscures it' and would advance 'fortified by moral enthusiasm of free people everywhere', and he ended with imagery from the Book of Solomon: 'fair as the moon, clear as the sun, and terrible as an army in banners.'

For the next two weeks Bowman was entirely committed to university work, for the final term was well under way. However, on 12 May he then became ill: Mabel called in the doctor, who diagnosed pleurisy and ordered him to bed. A week later university classes finished and Archie, his condition having worsened, was still in bed. He had been unable to deliver his final lecture of the course, so he wrote a letter to the class:

> I shall consider this year's course in Moral Philosophy utterly vain and worthless unless in the years to come you shall find the principles which I have tried to expound in theory of some value for the grim and relentless business of actual living.
>
> I shall feel greatly rewarded if anything you have learned in this class, or anything which, as a result of stimulus, you have thought out for yourselves, will prove of service in your hour of need, and in that warfare from which there is no discharge – the moral life.

One of the students read the letter out to the class, and later came back to the house and told Mabel that it had been 'received with great enthusiasm'. He also brought with him a composite letter to Bowman from the class. Mabel noted in her diary: 'Brought letter back which we enjoyed.'

However, Archie had demanded too much of himself for too long, and now he was putting up a fight for his life; a fight that lasted four weeks. Mabel, the love of his life, nursed him. She daily kept a note of his condition. He was in pain a lot of the time; sometimes in great pain. Once when he tried to get out of bed, he collapsed. Yet when he was conscious his mind was clear. His brother Alex would look in on him from time to time, but Mabel noted that he said very little.

Then, in her note about Archie's condition on Thursday, 11 June, she wrote: 'he slept the whole night through.' Later that morning the university exam results were out and he was interested in them. Then for early Friday morning, the diary reads: 'Archie took sudden faltering turn. Called nurse, but too late. He died in my arms about 8 o'clock. Dr came but too late. Had sat beside him all night holding his hand and he had been so sweet to me.'

Chapter Eight

The Long Day's Task is Done

His was an extraordinarily integrated character, with a purity of motive and a singleness of purpose.

Norman Kemp Smith

In the days that followed, Mabel was taken aback by the magnitude of the response to Archie's death: 'hundreds and hundreds of letters poured in and cables from America and telegrams.' The *Glasgow Herald* carried what Mabel described as a 'beautiful tribute to my husband.' Other major newspapers followed with obituaries, and Arthur Karney, Bishop of Southampton, wrote to *The Times* with an appreciation about Bowman's work in the prison camps. Mail kept on streaming in: 'Letters coming in in shoals. What a revelation of Archie.'

The funeral service was held in the University Chapel. This was the university where Mabel and Archie began their journey together and this was where it ended. That night, Mabel wrote in her diary: 'my best-beloved was buried today.'

The next day she decided to talk to the children about some of the changes that would be necessary. Their father's death was hard for them; they were 'heart-broken.' Alastair was 13 and at secondary school. Ian had turned 21; he would be graduating with an Honours MA in a few weeks and had applied for a post in the Indian Civil Service. Maisie would be 20 in a few months; she was due to graduate in a year's time and she was seeing Robert Gillespie, a young lecturer in the Mathematics Department. It was serious, and Mabel knew that.

That same afternoon, Robert Gillespie called round. Mabel wrote in her diary: 'Gillespie came in and said he wanted Maisie. Maisie very definite, both quite sure. Better so perhaps. God bless them both.'

She was a widow, grieving the loss of her husband, her older two children were getting set to leave home, and she had to organize what had to be done to leave a tied house and buy another. A few months later, she was choosing wallpaper for a house she bought in the village of Torrance, about 8 miles from Glasgow.

In early 1937 Ian sailed for India, and at the end of June, Maisie and Robert were married in the University Chapel.

Then there was the legacy of Archie's unfinished work to be seen to. The only book that he completed and saw published was *The Absurdity of Christianity*, a short work published by SCM Press in 1931. He had begun what was clearly going to be a major philosophical work in Princeton after the war. However, with his heavy schedule of commitments, he had not the leisure time for private writing and so never completed the work to which he had given the provisional title of *Naturalism and the Supernatural*. At one point he conceived of it as a two-volume work. During the summers when he took the family on holiday in Canada, in Nova Scotia and in the Laurentian mountains, he made good progress on it and from time to time he kept Kemp Smith up to date on the direction he was taking. However, things slowed after he took on the role of chairman of the Philosophy Department, but in the years 1924–26, he wrote the first draft of the anthropological chapters he had been researching.

Princeton was where the book could have been completed though; he knew it, and it must have added to the stress he was under in 1925 when he received the call from Glasgow University. After he had gone through the throes of deciding whether to accept the offer from Glasgow, in a letter to Dr Jacobus, a trustee of Princeton University, he said:

> The truth is, I wanted to stay on in Princeton…where I had so many dear friends, and where the happiest years of my life had been passed. I could not contemplate a change without dismay. And I'll be bound to admit that you had persuaded me that there was a real call for me here. None the less, my conscience troubled me sorely. I thought of the old country, impoverished, economically crippled…and assailed by every spiritual danger.

As a result of devoting his time to his teaching and the causes he upheld, the only time he gave himself to work on the book in the Glasgow years was in 1929 when he was on six months' leave of absence and visiting lecturer at the University of California at Berkeley and during those months he made progress on it. Then in 1932 came the invitation to deliver the Vanuxem lectures in 1934 and that meant another book. His health broke down, yet he wrote detailed notes for the series of six lectures and he was able to carry out the lecturing commitment but the book that was to follow had still to be written.

His friend Norman Kemp Smith discussed with Mabel the option of his taking up the task of editing the chapters that Archie had written all those years earlier and publishing it in Archie's name. This was what happened. Kemp Smith gave it the title *Studies in the Philosophy of Religion*. Mabel proof-read the manuscript and Kemp Smith wrote a 'Memorial Introduction' to it and it was published by Macmillan in 1938.

John Waugh Scott, Professor of Logic and Moral Philosophy at University College, Cardiff, who had been a lecturer at Glasgow University from 1905–20, was able to edit the text from Bowman's copious and clearly set out notes for the Vanuxem lectures, and it was published under the title *A Sacramental Universe* by Princeton University Press in 1939. So his major philosophical works were published posthumously.

Within Glasgow University, recognition of Bowman as an outstanding teacher was marked, and here his students and former students took over. In the academic session after Bowman's death, one of his former students founded the Bowman Medal in his memory. The medal was to be awarded annually to the most distinguished student in the Ordinary Class of Moral Philosophy.

The following year, in October 1938, Mabel, Maisie, Robert and Alastair were in the audience when Norman Kemp Smith unveiled the Bowman Plaque in the classroom where Bowman used to teach. It was an official university ceremony with the chancellor of the university and the principal in attendance, and it took place before an audience of students, staff, families and friends. Funding for the plaque had been raised by subscription from Bowman's students and friends.

Just what was there about Bowman's teaching that made students want to commemorate him and have a symbol of him displayed in his classroom for future generations? To most students coming up to university Moral Philosophy was an unknown and a bit of a bind that had to be taken in order to graduate for the broad-based curriculum of the MA degree.

Yet by 1928, Bowman's Ordinary Class in Moral Philosophy had grown in such numbers – in the year of his death it was 320 (it had been as high as 450 until the university cut back student intake) – that he had to divide it into two sections: he taught one section from 10.00 am to 11.00 am and the other from 11.00 am to 12 noon, and two days a week he met the Honours Class from 9.00 am to 10.00 am. Three solid hours of lecturing!

Kemp Smith included in his 'Memorial Introduction' to *Studies in the Philosophy of Religion* the account one of Bowman's students of the 1932–33 Ordinary Class gave about his style of teaching: Professor Bowman did not attempt to gain their favour at the start, according to the student; he began in a low key, giving them for the first few days a philosophic vocabulary, but then

> the flat land began to be left behind, the scene became rich and varied. He would explore enticing by-paths in physics, psychology and anthropology, that were as fascinating as the main topic of discussion. The highway to which he ever returned was nothing less than a search for a policy of life.

He varied his style between the serious and the light, and he took many of his illustrations from his own experience:

With perfect modesty he told us of events in his life, and what they meant to his philosophy. Thus we came to feel that we knew him intimately and had shared his travels and his prison-camp sufferings. At times he presented his class with a picture of himself in the most incongruous situations or unexpected places (I remember Hollywood as one of them), and asked us to laugh at him with him. It was a voluntary relinquishment of professorial dignity, that brought in a rich harvest of affection, breaking down the defences of the more cynical of his hearers, and completely disarming the jesters of the class. If at the start the members of the class were alike in that they were vague as to what Moral Philosophy was, and most of them decidedly lukewarm in their desire to know, by the end of the session, when the magic lectures were over, they were equally alike in feeling that they would never completely forget the clearer air and bright clime through which they had made their philosophic pilgrimage.

In the same classroom where the students made their philosophic pilgrimage, Norman Kemp Smith rose to give the eulogy that October day in 1938. No one could have been better suited to this. Kemp Smith had known him as student, colleague and friend. He touched lightly on the hardships of Bowman's early years: 'There was certainly not any nepotism in the Providence that arranged the external circumstances of his life.'

He spoke at greater length of the transformational effect of the prison camps on the man: discovering the impact he could make beyond the world of academe and the collection of poems he was able to write in those conditions, *Sonnets from a Prison Camp*, and the 'light they cast upon the mind and spirit of the author.' He spoke too of the 'deep impression' Bowman made on his return to Princeton in 1919; it was no exaggeration, Kemp Smith said, 'to say that he had come to be idolized in the community.'

Then Kemp Smith turned to the Glasgow years. Bowman's first commitment was to his teaching, but he found the time and energy to make an impact on the wider community through his commitment to a number of good causes, especially the cause of peace. Kemp Smith said that he doubted that even Bowman's closest friends and colleagues realized the strain he had put himself under through his level of commitment.

A sceptic in the audience might have tuned in at the words about the cause of peace and mused that only days had passed since the infamous 30 September Munich Agreement – in which Britain and France forced the democratic republic of Czechoslovakia to surrender part of Bohemia to Adolf Hitler's Thousand Year Reich – and that, in effect, Bowman's efforts on behalf of the ideal of the League of Nations had amounted to little more than idle chatter.

However, that assessment would have been wide of the mark. Bowman had not faced a defeat of the spirit, he would not have been disillusioned and given up at the Munich betrayal; he expected setbacks to the work of the League. He would have scourged the British government in print. This is what Winston Churchill did after Munich. Churchill was a discordant voice in the House of Commons amid the praise offered from all sides to Prime Minister Neville Chamberlain and he rose and said, amid interruptions, 'We have sustained a total and unmitigated defeat.' These words echoed what Bowman said in that same Palace of Westminster in 1931 in his address to Glasgow MPs:

> The point has been reached at which another failure would so impair the prestige of the League of Nations as to render its survival problematic. That is a contingency which would be too terrible to contemplate. Its effects upon every one of the nations involved would be tantamount to that of a crushing defeat in war.

However, he would have continued to strive for the ideal while accepting, when it came to the bit, the need to fight a just war. That is the way Norman Kemp Smith read Bowman too:

> He was in no danger of being disillusioned by the difficulties and the temporary defeats which from the start he foresaw as inevitable in the pursuit of the League of Nations ideal. But it had no more ardent and convinced supporter. It was chief among the causes in which he spent himself, in spendthrift fashion, in his last years.

Had Bowman lived a few more years, the creation of a new world organization would have been under way to replace the old, an organization that would have more powers and be potentially more effective than the old: the United Nations.

Then, before asking the principal to accept the plaque from Professor Bowman's students and friends, Kemp Smith alluded to Bowman's two major books, and by this time Kemp Smith had already completed his editing of *Studies in the Philosophy of Religion*.

'It is tragic that both works should have been left in some degree incomplete. What might he not have done had he enjoyed ten or twenty more years of good work?' He went on to say that the memorial plaque he was about to unveil would be 'a permanent memorial to show to the generations that will follow us what manner of man he was.'

Bowman's completion of his two major works would have been contingent on other factors too. Back in 1930, when he explained to President Hibben of

Princeton why he could not take up the university's offer of a professorship – although it was really the life he would have wanted – he put it thus:

> I can only say that the considerations that led me to return to Scotland in 1926 are even more pressing today… It is simply a case of the greatest need. I can never forget how when the war broke out you divined what must be passing in my mind, and in words of sympathetic understanding, offered me the release for which I longed but hardly dared to ask. Only, this new war which has begun is one which will last my lifetime, and in which I am much better qualified to render effective service.

Further back still, when he was in Hesepe prison camp, Archie began a sequence of four sonnets on 23 June 1918 and he put them under a section he called *Interlude*; he had then completed his 100th sonnet. At this point, he pauses and reflects on the 'sonnet chain' on which he has worked, and he uses the image of an artisan, a smith, stepping back to scrutinize the shape he is giving to the artefact he is creating. Then the poet moves from 'the dreams' of poetry and creativity and on to day-to-day life where neither 'chance nor inspiration can fulfil / The welded whole' but 'man's more sovereign Will.' Then in the last of the group he writes:

> IV
> So forward still, might but my strength avail
> Out of the brooding darkness of my plight,
> Each day to bring one glimmering shaft of light,
> Each night to add some fragment to the tale,
> That so I sleep. Else o'er my dreams prevail
> These sorrows, or within me hour-long smite
> The hammers of the brain, and turn the night
> Into a thing to make man's reason fail.
> – A little further; for the thoughts still rise
> Over me like a soughing wind, that blows
> From where the surges boom along the graile
> Of the world's misery under lowering skies,
> – A little further and my task I close,
> Lest twilight overtake me and I stale.

By the time twilight overtook Archie Bowman, he had not closed his task and in committing himself wholly to it he had burned all his candles right down, but as darkness gathered, he was granted a gentle death in the arms of his love 'for this life & forever.'

Epilogue

Less than a year after the unveiling of the Bowman Plaque, war was declared. Bowman's sons and his son-in-law served in it, and Mabel and Maisie involved themselves in voluntary work.

Clydeside was a target for enemy bombing, so Maisie moved out to the village of Torrance and stayed with Mabel for most of the war years, and during those years Maisie had three children. Robert was serving in the RAF; he was stationed at the RAF Air Traffic Control Unit, Prestwick and whenever he had a forty-eight-hour pass, he was able to join the family. Then for a time Maisie rented accommodation at Prestwick, but she was in touch with her mother regularly and on 12 June 1942 her letter to Mabel began:

> Dearest Mother
> We have been thinking about you all day today. It seems almost unbelievable that it is six whole years since Daddy died – he still seems so vividly and intensely alive, but then I expect he will never cease being that to us. You will be feeling so sad tonight and I just hate to think of you being alone.

As the war extended and Japan joined the Axis, India became a theatre of operations and Ian took part in the Lushai Hills Total Defence Scheme.

Alastair joined the RAF and trained as a pilot. He was posted to Transport Command. In 1943, he was flying Catalina seaplanes from Pensacola in Florida to the west coast of Scotland, to Oban bay.

Mabel went through the same anxieties and fears as in the Great War. In that war, as the casualty lists appeared daily, Mabel once said to Archie: 'I think I'm sorriest though for the young lads who have fallen just as they were bursting into manhood.' Her son Alastair was only 20 years of age when the shadow of death darkened her home. The dreaded telegram arrived: 'Regret to inform you that your son Flying Officer Alastair Allan Stewart Bowman is missing and believed to have lost his life as a result of air operations on 4th November 1943.' There was no misinformation about this telegram as there had been about Archie's fate all those years ago. She felt her son's death very keenly.

She had lost her younger son and she had not seen her older son for years, but when peace came, Mabel set sail for India for a long vacation at Ian's. It turned out not as she expected: she was an active and independent woman, and she was bored for there were house servants to do what she would normally busy herself with. She felt guilty too because Maisie was going to have a fourth child, and Mabel felt she should have been there to give support.

In one of his last letters to Kemp Smith before he left Princeton for Glasgow, Archie had formed the view that Britain's role as a great power was on the wane then, that its commercial and political power over India could not continue. That duly came about in 1947, when India became independent. The Indian Civil Service was dismembered and reformed, and with the departure of the British, Ian left and returned to Scotland.

It was a gloomy post-war Britain to which he returned; there was a severe winter of 1946/47 that led to coal shortages. Ian had his father's sense of serving the common good and he became a coal miner; he worked down the pits at Balmore Colliery for about three months, coming home each evening grime-encrusted. Then he spent a short time in Manchester making use of his administrative skills during the setting up of Keele University. Following this he took up post as an assistant registrar at University College in Ibadan, Nigeria. However, the days of expats working in senior positions in the British colonies were numbered and Ian returned to the UK.

Married with two children and the career path he had chosen petering out, Ian decided on a career change. He went to teacher training college and, following this, he first taught Classics in a secondary school in Glasgow, but then went on to Falkirk Technical College where he taught Liberal Studies. In later years, Ian wrote several chapters for a biography of his father but it was not completed. However, he wrote an article on his father's philosophy (see Appendix III).

To mark the fifth centenary of the foundation of the University of Glasgow, a series of lectures was held in the university and published, in 1952, under the title *Fortuna Domus*. Professor C.A. Campbell contributed the chapter on the history of Philosophy at the university, and when he dealt with the recent past, A.A. Bowman was given centre stage. Campbell felt that some of Bowman's chapters of *A Sacramental Universe* 'contain some of the finest philosophical writing of recent times.' Also Campbell judged that in the classroom Bowman's influence on his students 'cannot often have been surpassed in the annals of the University.'

The nature of the friendships Archie had had with contemporaries was long-lasting. The bonding between Archie and Norman Kemp Smith stretched into the next generation: Maisie had become a close friend of Kemp Smith's daughter Janet, and the link held when Maisie took her four children to Janet's daughter's wedding.

The friendship that had begun in the Princeton years between the Bowmans and the Hendels lasted long after Archie's death. Charles Hendel came to Glasgow in 1962 to give the Gifford Lectures; he and his wife visited Mabel, who was by then staying with Maisie and her family. Charles Hendel had also been responsible for editing and republishing in the United States, in 1958, *The Absurdity of Christianity* in which he included essays that Archie had written.

Mabel, always strong and resilient, became a haven for her grandchildren; she was very important to them in their young lives, interested in them and supportive in whatever they were doing, and she was non-judgemental. She had a small car, and when they were teenagers they learned to drive in it. Independent for years, at the age of 70 Mabel suffered a stroke that partly paralysed her right side, but she did not accept defeat and she taught herself to write with her left hand.

A supporter of the CND movement, Mabel subscribed to the publication *Peace News*, the official paper of the Peace Pledge Union, and she went on 'Ban the Bomb' marches, walking, as it were, hand-in-hand with Archie. Many years after their first walk together as a couple, she had told him: 'What a long, long walk it was that first night and it wasn't half long enough. All the years that have passed haven't been half long enough either. I think we could walk on for ever together and still be unsatisfied.'

Mabel died in 1967, aged 79, and in her will she made a bequest of the Bowman Prize to be awarded annually, along with the Bowman Medal, to the most distinguished student in the Ordinary Class of Moral Philosophy at Glasgow University.

Afterword

As the eldest surviving grandchild of Archibald Allan Bowman, perhaps it is appropriate that I have the privilege of writing a few words as an afterword to this book of significant importance.

Although we never actually met our grandfather, he had a strong influence during the years that we were growing up in the west end of Glasgow. We were always aware of his commitment to duty and of the deep love and family values that he shared with our grandmother, his beloved wife Mabel.

His belief in a 'Just War' is of paramount importance when considering his contribution to and involvement in the First World War. His commitment to duty and to friendship was evident right up to his last few days. Owing to his wartime experiences and possibly also to the fact that he had suffered from nephritis as a young child, he was never a strong man. From letters written by Mabel describing the details of his passing we are able to ascertain that some weeks before he died he had contracted pneumonia from which he was slowly recovering. However, although still unwell, he dutifully attended the funeral of a close colleague at which he got soaked from standing in heavy rain. His pneumonia returned with a vengeance and he passed away several days later.

After Archie's death Mabel had to leave the home in the quadrangle at the university. The family moved to the village of Torrance just outside Glasgow to a delightful stone-built detached house called Rosebank Cottage. Although smaller than 4 The University, this house quickly became an open home where family and friends were always welcome. Mabel integrated into village life, attending church, joining many local organizations and even teaching at the village school for some years.

These years were, on the whole, busy happy years for Mabel. Sadly, tragedy struck the family when Alastair, who had joined the RAF in October 1941, was killed. Mabel was devastated by his death but bravely continued her busy life being supported by her large family connections and many friends.

Although warfare was certainly not part of the family ethos, there obviously existed the doctrine of a moral duty to support rightful causes. Archie Bowman had instilled into his family the importance of supporting 'just movements', however abhorrent the circumstances. At the end of the war Mabel spent a year in India living with Ian. Archie and Mabel both had a love of travel and were always interested in other countries and culture. From a very early age railways had fascinated Archie and perhaps this interest was manifested in his delight in travelling in foreign lands. The many letters that Mabel wrote to Maisie from India indicate the great interest that she took in the Indian lifestyle and the political situation of the time.

On returning from India Mabel again took up residence in Torrance where she spent many happy and busy years. We as children have so many good memories of visiting Rosebank Cottage. She was certainly a very talented 'hands-on' grandmother. We never actually perceived her as a granny and we called her by the name of 'Biddy'. She had many skills, demonstrated by her excellent ability to cook, bake and knit, and she was also a keen gardener. She also took a great interest in current affairs, with political discussion always being a challenge. She had the ability to make everyone feel welcome. Rosebank Cottage was certainly an exciting place to visit in those days. 'Biddy' was a person who naturally enjoyed life and encouraged those around her to have fun. She liked a challenge and, being an enthusiastic bridge-player, cards played a role in our childhood years. Perhaps it was her outgoing nature that was one of the reasons that the somewhat shy and reserved Archie found her so admirable.

Notwithstanding her increasing age, she still managed to be an influence in our teenage years and we were aware that, although she seldom mentioned him, the memory of her life with Archie was still of great significance. Mabel died in May 1967, but her memory, love and influence will always be with us.

Mabel's time with Archie Bowman undoubtedly comprised the most notable years of her life. She has bequeathed to us the memory of a charismatic man of strong theological views. His lectures were famous and were so popular that there was often standing room only. Mabel was the support and practical influence in the life of this academic and spiritual man. He was at heart a pacifist and his legacy of peace lived on in his widow who was a strong supporter of pacifism, and in the 1960s took part in a 'Ban the Bomb' march.

Being the eldest of five children, Archibald Bowman developed a deep sense of responsibility early in life and, as a son of the Manse, he had a deep faith with strong theological views. In some respects his approach to religion and church traditions was unconventional. He saw little point in christening young children and believed that baptism should be for those who have faith in Jesus. This excluded the baptism of underage children and hence as his descendants we were not christened as children. Although nowadays this would not be an unusual circumstance, it certainly was when we were young. Church membership would appear to be an issue of which he also had deep theological views and we are led to believe that he questioned the moral values of membership. He shrank from the concept of communion, as practised in Scottish churches.

Afterword

I would like to mention the great debt we owe to the extensive details of the life of Archibald Allan Bowman as documented by my uncle, Ian Bowman, and we are also indebted to my mother and to Archie's widow Mabel for having the insight to store the massive amount of family correspondence and archives that we have now inherited.

Marjorie Stewart
June 2017

Appendix I

The Christ of Mory

(February, 1918)

Day dwindled. On the gray-green upland hung
The still and heavy fore-spring afternoon,
A tepid season, when the spirit takes
A sense of pause in nature, as the year
Like some great pendulum with solemn swing
Slows to a stop on turning. Bush nor tree
Showed bursting bud, nor greening of the bark,
That comes before the greening of the leaf –
A melancholy fallow interval
Sundering the seasons.

In like fallow mood
I sauntered from Behagnies. Nothing stirred
On all the landscape round but one lone wain
Leisurely heading with me to the east
Upon the beaten soft fair-weather track,
Half a mile off upon the plateau's rim.
It was a place of grassy stretches bare,
Such as in stricken Picardy this day
May everywhere be seen, dead, colourless,
Unfeatured and obscure, yet sauturate
With the tremendous presence of events
Hot and reverberating from the hand
Of the Dispenser; steeped too in the sense
Of something brewing and about to be.
Behind me like a ribbon, league by league,
Unwound in weary undulating lengths,
Straight as a die and pulsing with the flow
Of never-ending traffic, south and north,
A broad unrutted artery of war,
The dusty, wheel-worn, roaring Arras road.

There on the hog-back to my left and rear,
Jagged and gaunt against the flushing gray,
Ervillers rises, broken on the sky,
A place of gables, where on many a clear
And bitter night of winter steely stars
Sparkled into interiors, and the winds
That bear the snow out of the frozen north,
Whimpered and soughed around extinguished hearths.
Upon my right, beyond the ridge whose trees
Define its course, a little to the south
Of where it dips and rises near the place
That used to be Sapignies, still so called,
Lies Bapaume, now a humped and crumpled pile,
Yet surging with a feverish after-life,
While congregating waggons, massing men
Lend to this graveyard purlieu the brisk air
Of war's peculiar cheerfulness – a forge
Of destiny for men as yet unborn.
For here converge the fateful highways three,
Each ending in a haunted battleground;
Ill-boding Cambrai, where is Bourlon Wood;
The steppes of Arras, falling towards the north
To Fampoux's dark canal, and overlooked
By that doomed eminence where Monchy takes
Daily upon her torn and scorching brow
The salt of pitiless and scathing fire.
Lastly the road that leads by Warlencourt
To Albert and the sour and marish tract
That opens darkly with the sombre fen
Of Thiepval, where the sobbing Ancre strains
Its melancholy way from pool to pool
Among stripped woods about the pitted face
Of that low land; and war's receding tide
Leaves to deep silence and the drilling worm
The solemn secrets of the vast and mourne
Battlefield of the Somme.

Around my steps,
As I went pondering, gathered here and there
A tangled mass of those becoloured strands

That cumber backward areas, and my feet
Once and again took shipwreck in the toils.
Here grass-grown trench decayed and derelict wire
Marked the old line, and pickets half-unscrewed,
Rusty and bent and leaning towards the ground,
Unable to sustain the web of barbed
And twisted filigree, that lay collapsed
In straggling wisps and bunches all around.
Ahead upon the scarred and sifted ridge
That towards the east the whole horizon bounds,
Clusters the wooden huts, 'mid whose low roofs
A heap of mottled gray, and in between
Some red-tiled steading towering over all –

The ruin at this distance undiscerned –
Abbey and village, cheerless Mory stood.
Now past the fault that splits the slope in twain,
Along the scour and by the sunken road,
And down into the hollow, where the mud
Lay like a bank of silt, at length I came
Out of the rising way beyond, to where
They water the draught-horses. On the left
Abruptly from the roadway rose the wrecked
And desecrated graveyard, and the shell
Of what in other times had been the place
Apart and consecrate, where Mory paid
Her vows to the Creator. Something stirred
Within me, and I leapt the wall and stood
Among the tombstones. All around displaced
Lay the fond and beaded wreathes
That love had laid to love with tender hands
And streaming eyes in those great opening days
When France sustained the onfall of the war,
And every village, cluster of small farms,
Sent up its handful, till that hour unnamed,
To the Immortals, named among them now.
But not on those my thought dwelt as I stood
And marked the ruin of their sepulture.
Rather I wondered what had since befallen
Those whom they left, the steadfast gray old men,

And the gnarled mothers, crooked with the toil
Of long brave lives, and the young wives, whose hearts,
Helped by the unrealizing eagerness
Of children's hands, had planned and planted there
That tasteless, touching, tender symbolism,
Infinitely pathetic, since it speaks
The eternal Inexpressible of grief.
Where are they, those who waited, watched and wept,
Where are they, whose familiar human warmth
Made of these stones the sanctity of home?
– Now blown about the land, or run to earth
In some strange ground that nothing can redeem
To what with these neglected graves is gone
For ever from them?

There rose a mound,
A ghostly thing, six metres high, compact
Of stones and rubble, wreckage of the church,
And on the peak, an insolence of war,
From its bent staff a rag of white and red
Hung drooping in the still oppressive air.
To this I mounted, scarcely knowing why,
Idly contemplative, with life enough
Only to nurse the emotions of the hour,
The sadness and the killing loneliness,
The sense of what had been, the brooding sense
Of what might yet be, and feverish lull
Between the storms. It was as if War slept,
While in and out between its massive limbs,
And round its ponderous head unhelmeted,
Horses and men and wagons wound about
Upon their little business. On their arms the
The Great Powers rested.

As I stood and gazed
Upon the desolation at my feet,
Extending thence to the horizon's rim,
My eyes alit upon the crucifix,
Which to my level and a little more

The Christ of Mory

Rose shapely, modelled to the life, but worn
And weathered. By one arm Our Saviour hung;
The other by some chance of war dislodged
And seeming as if asking for its nail,
While pitifully those pierced feet askew
Sought in the air some resting place in vain.
Gently the figure swayed, and now and then
A sparrow perched upon the thorn-crowned head. –
The melancholy spirit of the scene
Deepened upon me. Not a foot of ground
On all that landscape, not a garden-space,
Nor road nor bank nor clump of stunted bush,
Nor this familiar figure of God's Son,
But war had altered it, and lo, there loomed
A wilderness, manhandled to a stone.
Sounds rose at intervals. Upon the still
And falling twilight came the dull, clop, clop
Of horses' hooves with pause, and soon the splash
And lapping of the water, and the soft
Blast of dilating nostrils o'er the trough.
A bugle sang to cookhouse on the hill.
The hour was five o'clock.

I could not see
That ignominy but it spoke the choice
And judgment of the ages. Him of whom
They made a Roman criminal and set
Upon a cross to worship, now they shoot
Down from that cross, while once again they add
Insult to crucifixion – the great Sign
That sealed the front of centuries become
The jest of field-guns. So the world is purged
Of the supreme hypocrisy, the cross
Thenceforth the symbol of the irony
Of twice a thousand years. No knee will bend
From this day on for ever, no head bow
But in derision to this effigy
Of a rejected god, no hand be found
To set Christ up upon His cross again.

Over the hill a spiral of blue smoke
Tempted me with the vision of the cheer
Of many a winter evening fetely spent
Among my comrades, when we sat and talked
The long night out by flickering candlelight,
While frozen twigs, that lent a look of warmth,
Spat in the brazier, and the crusted rime
Sparkled upon the corrugated roof
And guttered into drops. I turned to go,
The prospect swarming on me like a dream,
In its stark rawness hideous. Something moved
Out of dead space. The rag of white and red
Shivered a little, and the wisp of smoke,
As if beneath some ceiling of the air,
Floated to southward. Christ creaked on his nail.
Suddenly nature softened, and there came
A look upon her like the gradual smile
That overspreads the face of one who dreams
A happy dream; while in the lifting west
The cloud-gates parted wide, and burst
Upon the world a majesty of light,
White-cored and shafted and unbearable,
Lining the cumulus, and through the vast
And blinding sky-space, striking for the height
Of mid-most heaven, where molten gold dispersed
In luminous dusk, grew pale and dwindling out
In golden-green and olive, faint sea-blue,
And purpling vapour shot with drifting fire.
One moment on the rim of earth the sun
Rested his glory insupportable,
And wrought transfiguration. Time told out
The meted span. Earth's breathless circle hung
Upon his going, and the spacious west
Vibrated to the passage of his fire.
Softly he settled, softly slipped away,
And where the splendour vanished gradual eve
Trod out the embers, and the twilight fell.
– But not before that radiance had revealed
A secret to my soul. For as the sun
Sank in the west, there came a lone white beam

Out of his core of brightness, quivering, slow,
And most divinely pure, and resting, dwelt
Upon the Presence, and the Thing became
A second Glory and a living form,
Shockingly real. Art doth not aspire
To such a semblance of unfrozen grief,
Statured in palpating wood. I felt
At length the yearning of the soul of France,
In thrice ten thousand villages unsealed,
A deep dark fountain wheresoe'er these Christs
Sprinkled her face with agony and hope.
Here is the port, I felt, to which they come,
The last word in them, brief epitome
Of all they are, these steadfast gray old men,
And crooked women faithful to their toil,
And patient of their portion, versed in grief,
Yet unsubdued, and loyal to their age,
And to fair France. So is their country judged,
And with their land themselves – by this dead Thing
Touched into life by Sunlight.

Then it came
Upon me strangely that Christ's image hung,
Although the sun had died on ridge and plain,
Translucent in the deepening twilight, lit
As by some incandescence of its own,
Rising and sinking like the flame that bathes
In muffled fire a lantern's cheeks of horn.
The very roots shook in me, and my heart
Went like a water-hammer, while the last
Faint vestige of the beam strained slowly by
Instinct with Life, and seemed to find its way
Into the Thing that held me. Day was gone
On village and on field, and sacred night
Found me beneath the mounting of the stars
Face to face with this Fear. My blood ran cold,
And terror of Transfiguration numbed
My conscience like a nightmare. I had marked
The look of spirit in that painted eye,
And on those carven lips there came what seemed

A parting as for speech. The illusion held
One moment only, and my heart returned
Into its seat. Yet in that moment's space
The elemental in me loosed the shaft
Of judgement o'er the desolated world,
And like a wind of heaven the solemn truth
Bore down upon my soul.

Rejected? Yes
For twice a thousand years – and this the end!
This battle-wilderness, this overthrow
Of the whole race of man by this one Man,
Named of the sorrows and the long despite
That having nailed, half shakes Him from His tree –
This pitiful and dangling form that gropes
To find its way back to its nail again!
So while man will not, while the world rejects,
<u>He</u> judgeth, salting the whole world with fire,
And judging, <u>liveth</u>; living, perfecteth
His triumph over Time; and triumphing,
Reveals the Timeless, that which hath not moved
From the Beginning, when the Word became
The flesh men crucified – the Law that stands
At the dividing of the ways, and looms
Behind the generations, sundering
The ever-lasting Opposites; that crouched
Awaiting the creation, when the face
Of the dark deep first shivered into life,
And on the finger of Jehovah spun
This beautiful doomed earth; the steadfast Law
That moved not when the new-born light of day
Sparkled upon the snow of Ararat,
And made a glowing garden of the Lord
Among the rivers, till the hour it heard
Sin shake creation, undisturbed the while;
Unmoved when on the face of the green earth
The flood welled and subsided, Sodom took
The scathe of brimstone; Babel rose and fell,
Egypt and Nineveh and Babylon
Passed like a dream, and Rome and Israel

Divided man's inheritance; unmoved
At that supremest moment of all time,
That sundered Time in two, and rent the Veil
From top to bottom. 'Tis the Law that stands
Behind the slaughter, and above the noise
Of hate, beneath the silence of despair
Works all these changes, changeless, and prevails,
Allotting each his portion, life or death.
So whether life hath issue, 'tis the Law,
And whether death, it is the Law convicts
Of righteousness and judgment – righteousness,
That will not fail on earth while death and sin
Go hand in hand and judgement purifies.
– Yet is the bitter tale but half told out;
For while the Law prevails, and while the Right
Fails not upon the earth and will not fail,
The kingdom tarries. Twice a thousand years,
And still man waits its advent; still man asks
Will this world see its dawn? 'Tis not enough
To know that the Law triumphs over Time;
Have the Time-born no triumph? Must we bear
Through all the generations that first curse,
Handing down sin with death from sire to son,
Till the earth melt in fire? – No answer came
Out of the infinite of space. The Star
Of Eve set voiceless; and the Pleiades
Swung blindly on, fulfilling but the Law;
While out of time there came the mocking laugh
Of the two thousand years. My heart went sick
With anguish at the thought – when there befell
A thing incredible.

Upon the nail
The Christ-Thing moved, and ere my sudden cry
Escaped into the night, I felt once more
A living eye upon me, such an eye
As on that night the appalled denier saw
Slowly to fix and yearningly to dwell
Upon him with unutterable ruth,
And the cock crew. I felt upon my face

The effulgence of a light that never dawned
Nor set on earth or ocean, and words came,
Words in that voice ineffable that last
Was on the highway to Damascus heard.

'And if I tarry, what is that to thee?
Fulfil thine own brief passion. Mine abides
His perfect Will. The cup remains with me.
And if from man the Perfect Wisdom hides
The hour when the cup passeth, dost thou think
Salvation passeth also? – Lo, I drink!
Behold these wounds. I tarry on my tree.'

The voice was still. Upon my face I lay,
How long I know not. One thought held my soul.
He still abides his Passion, and with Him
This generation for the ages drinks
Its smaller portion. Deeply let it drink,
That the cup pass not till the Father's will
In us too is complete. My soul be firm.
Behold thy God! He tarries on his tree!

At length I went. The heavens above were white
With flocks of stars; and on the face of night
Into the eastern sky-space quivering rose,
Expanded, lingered, turned and slowly sank
The opening Very light over Bullecourt.

Hesepe, 15th August.

Appendix II

The Chestnuts

'Twas on a bright May morning,
When the sun began to shine,
They marched us out in column-of-route
From Rastatt by the Rhine.

'Twas from the Russian Lager[1]
The columned march began.
Beside each squad moved like a cloud
A sullen bayonet-man.

The spring upon our spirits
Renewed her ancient spell,
When suddenly before us frowned
The grim old Citadel.

One moment gloomed above us
The portal's ancient night;
The next upon our eyes there burst
A wonder of the light.

For suns of May had quickened
Old Friedrichfeste's gloom,
And on the chestnuts thickened
Their hyacinthine bloom.

And I saw the apple-blossoms
Come crowding to my door
In an orchard over the ocean,
My orchard now no more.

---

1. One of the two prisoner-of-war camps at Rastatt, the other being the Citadel of Friedrichfeste, which is the scene of the brief vision. The chestnuts growing round the barrack square were among the finest I have ever seen. A.A.B.

Appendix III

A Voice from the Past

Professor Archibald Allan Bowman
by Ian Bowman

The following is an edited version of a paper written by Ian Bowman about his father.

Professor Archibald Allan Bowman was Professor of Moral Philosophy at Glasgow University from 1927 to 1936. In that short period he added great distinction to a Chair already made illustrious by Francis Hutcheson, Adam Smith, Thomas Reid, Edward Caird and Sir Henry Jones. With his friend and colleague Norman Kemp Smith of Edinburgh University, he brought Scottish philosophy to a dimension it had not touched since the eighteenth century and which has not been equalled in subsequent years. He and Kemp Smith mustered formidable powers of intellect and scholarship to challenge the negative, limited quality of so much of the philosophical thinking of their day, reviving in their own way the spirit of the Scottish Enlightenment.

However, Bowman did not confine his powers to academic scholarship and contests. He went out into the world and tackled major problems of society: the problem of creating a lasting world peace, of sustaining the morale of populations hit by world recession, of eradicating social evils. His approach to these problems – which are still with us today, more intense than ever – was an expression of his philosophical thinking, applied in a practical manner and expounded with a clarity of reasoning and a sympathy for the human predicament which brought understanding and encouragement to those involved in it. It carried a message of hope, for Bowman was a great optimist, and by the lucid reasoning of his arguments it created confidence that the things hoped for were realizable. It was essentially an expression of faith in the ability of spiritual strength to resolve the problems of the human predicament.

During his tenure of the Chair in Glasgow his words made an impact throughout Scotland and well beyond it, so that his sudden and premature death in 1936 was noted with regret and respect for his memory in every continent of the world. However, the posthumous publication of the two major statements of his philosophy in *A Sacramental Universe* and *Studies in the Philosophy of Religion* were overshadowed by the outbreak of the Second World War and the potential impact of the books was swept aside in the headlong confusion of world events. By the time that confusion had been dealt with and a semblance of world peace restored, a new order of society was emerging and Bowman's thoughts and teaching were largely ignored by generations to whom, at best, he was only a name. Today, when human society is faced with a prospect of deepening gloom, despondency and danger, it might be profitable to try to assess his attitude to the sort of problems that beset us and to see whether his teaching carries any message that might help us to resolve them.

Bowman's philosophy is a meticulously thorough investigation into what it means to be a human being. 'In the person of man,' he wrote, 'two orders of being meet – the order of eternity and the order of nature. Between these two there is apparent antipathy. Their relation is one of perpetual tension. This is the supreme predicament of human life.' The order of nature is the physical mode of being in its relation to a conscious subject. The physical mode, in the ultimate analysis, is simply a vibratory system whose reality is shown in the fact that the vibrations are measurable in terms of space and time. It exists in a universal scheme of being that contains also the spiritual mode of existence, separate from the physical mode but able to affect it and to transform it into what Bowman describes as the natural mode:

> In the presence of spirit nature becomes alive. At the touch of a percipient organism it contracts new meanings, it bursts into new manifestations. Vibrations become colours and sounds. Space begins to glow and to throb. Power and action assume new forms. What we call value suddenly appears. Utility gives a new significance to nature's aimless process. Beauty unveils its face. And in the midst of this dynamic transformation stands the transformer, man...

It is in man that the two orders meet, and it is through man that the transformation takes place by the impact of his consciousness, a function of the spiritual order, upon the vibratory system of the physical order.

An important feature of this transformation is in the sphere of time. The time of physical events is characterized by successiveness. Every event is prior to some events and subsequent to others. However, we cannot say that it is past, present or future, for past and future require a reference point which is the 'now', the present, and this does not exist in the physical order of being, whereas 'before' and 'after' define themselves directly against one another. The 'now' which is present time exists only in the experience of the conscious subject. If we apply the distinction of past, present and future to events in the physical order of being, we do so by considering them not only in relation to each other, but also in relation to our experience of them. In doing so, we are passing from the purely physical order to a new order in which the physical, as the natural, comes together with the spirit in a system whose principles are determined by the constitution of spirit.

This present, which is a function of conscious experience, must not be thought of as a dividing line between past and future, but as an activity of consciousness in which the past and the future are related in one constantly unfolding matrix. It is what Bowman describes as 'a continuity of synthesis' of each with each. For the individual spirit the succession of experiences is accompanied by the experience of their succession. This experience is necessarily one. In its unity lies the self-identity of the spirit. Within it the components of the succession of experiences are changed in relation to it. Past is adjusted to future in the comprehensive present. A later phase in this time of the spirit not only *displaces* an earlier, but *transforms* it by incorporating it into itself, in a process which Bowman calls 'retroactivity'. However, in the continuity of synthesis each present experience becomes a past, relating to a subsequent present experience whose approaching presence can be deduced and for which some preparation can be made. We adjust to a future possibility in an attitude of anticipation. Since recognition is implied in our adjustment to the past, the future is as much a function of the ever-moving present as is the past. This anticipatory power in the spiritual mode is characteristic of the time of spirit which Bowman terms 'prolepsis'. In the specious present sustained by an act of synthesis embodying retroactivity and prolepsis, which Bowman calls 'Spirit-Time', the development of an integrated personality becomes possible.

Yet while this is a possibility, in practice the tensions between the natural and the spiritual in man too often result in the natural asserting itself and preventing the integration of the spirit, which instead succumbs to nature. This is not entirely unexpected under the limited conditions of our finitude. There is, however, a way whereby the power of spirit may be conserved against the disintegrating forces of the natural order. This rests in an adjustment of the conscious subject not merely to his own past and future, but to the eternal order that comprises every future and every past in the universal consciousness of the Divine Being whom we call God:

> He is the divine co-consciousness compresent with us in the inwardness of our subjectivity. To realize that God knows us *from within*, that his experience of us includes our experience of ourselves, is *to know God*: it is to realize the greatest of all possibilities open to man – a community of experience with the Divine.

In order to escape from the predicament brought about by the antipathy between the two orders of being in which he has a part, man must seek to know God. Through the knowledge of God, the creature of a day enters the order of eternity. This is the only activity capable of bringing about that full integration of personality that makes it possible for him to escape from his predicament.

Any attempt to summarize Bowman's closely-reasoned philosophy must be unsatisfactory. This brief statement can do little more than indicate the trend of his thinking and the emphasis that he placed on the importance of the spiritual order of being in the individual's attempt to resolve his predicament. Nothing in the natural order can do this. The materialistic activities of the pursuit of happiness and pleasure or the carrying through of projects are inadequate for the integration of personality. It is only in the seeking of community of experience with God that man can hope for its full integration. This experience is characterized by feelings of wonder and numinous fear which arouse in the seeker a sense of reverence for spirit. Reverence for spirit is the highest value in the human scale. It makes possible Christ's injunction that we should love our fellow men, even those whose actions are hostile to us. It is reverence for the individual as a spirit in the spiritual order of being that ought to guide all our human relationships.

Bowman's philosophy posited the need for relationships between individuals as an integral part of each individual's experience. With reverence for each individual as the highest value in his experience the theory can be translated into practical terms of international friendship between the groups that form nations. There is no moral justification for the violent hostilities of war when the experience of being a person, which all human beings have, of necessity includes the experience of a creaturely feeling for other individuals who are having their own experience of being a person. The message stands out clearly: that it is not by military might or political dogma that pacification of the world is to be obtained, but by the unloosening of the power of individual friendly relations on an international scale, controlled by reverence for human personality. In the context of today's world situation it implies a lifting of the curtains of suspicion and mistrust with which governments too often surround nations and the encouragement of natural friendship between peoples.

Bibliography

Primary sources (published works of A.A. Bowman):

(1919) *Sonnets from a Prison Camp* (John Lane, The Bodley Head, London)
(1921) 'The Chestnuts', *Princeton Alumni Weekly*, Vol. XXII, No. 10, 7 December
(1931) *The Absurdity of Christianity* (SCM Press, London)
(1938) *Studies in the Philosophy of Religion* (ed. Norman Kemp Smith) (Macmillan, London)
(1939) *A Sacramental Universe* (ed. John Waugh Scott) (Princeton University Press, Princeton, New Jersey)
(1958 edition) *The Absurdity of Christianity and other Essays* (ed. Charles W. Hendel) (The Liberal Arts Press, New York)

Secondary sources (newspapers and other publications):

Aberdeen Press and Journal
Beith Supplement and Advertiser
Evening Gazette
Free Press
Glasgow Evening Times
Glasgow Herald
Mind (journal)
New York Times
Peace News
Scots Observer
The Nation (journal)
The Scotsman
The Spectator (magazine)
The Times

Index

Aitken, Jennie, 10, 41-3, 60-1, 76, 80, 91-2
Anderson, Maj, 8-9
Argyle and Sutherland Highlanders, 24
Armentières, 43
Arras, 19,
Aubers, 32

Balliol College, 108
Beith, 4, 133
Beith Academy, 4
Berlin, 4, 72-3
Berles-au-Bois, 22
Biddel, Col, 89
Black Forest, 35
Bowman, Alastair (son of Archie and Mabel), 104, 124, 137, 139, 143, 147
Bowman, Alex (Archie's brother), 67, 69, 104, 132, 135
Bowman, Archibald, Allan (Archie),
 training officer, 7-15
 on active service, 17-30
 prisoner of war, 31-70
 with army of occupation, 71, 74-93
 return to Princeton University, 95-113
 at Glasgow University, 115-35
 commemorated, 120-34

Bowman, Arthur (Archie's brother), 5
Bowman, Daisy (Archie's sister), 41
Bowman, Ian (son of Archie and Mabel), 3, 12-14, 27, 31, 39-41, 43, 47, 61-2, 64, 68-70, 81-3, 105, 124, 137, 143-4, 147, 149, 163-6
Bowman, Jim (Archie's brother), 5, 104, 132
Bowman, Mabel (née Stewart) (wife of Archie)
 writes to Archie in prison camps, 40-8, 60-4
 writes to Archie in Cologne, 81-5, 91-3
Bowman, Maisie (daughter of Archie and Mabel), 11, 13-14, 27, 31, 37, 39-41, 43, 47, 61, 64, 68, 70, 81, 137, 139, 144, 149
British Army of the Rhine, 76, 94
British Prisoners of War Book Scheme, 65-6

Bross, William, 109
Bross Foundation Prize, 109-10

Calais, 25-6
Campaign for Nuclear Disarmament, 145
Catterick, 7-8
Chamberlain, Neville, (Prime Minister), 141
Churchill, Winston, 74, 141
Civil Permit Office, 76-7, 92
Cohen, Capt, 77
Cologne (Köln), 68-70, 74
Collins, Sir Godfrey, 129
Coolidge, Calvin (President of the United States), 105
Coopers the Grocers, 56
Cumbernauld, 77
Cuthbertson, Capt, 1, 27, 31, 36, 47-8
Czech Legions, 72

Davies, Sir Alfred, 65-6
Davis, Pen, 105-106
Denmark, 36
Divisions,
 3rd, 23
 40th, 24, 27, 41
 51st, 23
Dixon, William Macneile, 17, 40, 74, 93-4, 111
Duchess of Westminster, 23
Durham Light Infantry, 28

Educational Institute of Scotland (EIS), 117-18
Estaires, 27, 30, 43
Étaples, 23
Evening Times, 6

Faber, Maj, 64
Falkirk Technical College, 144
Farquharson, Gen, 9
Fite, Warren, 72, 85, 91, 93, 97-8, 100-101
Forbes, R F, Lt Col, 19
Fort de Mons, 33

Fortuna Domus, 144
Fournes, 33

Garratt, Capt, 89
Gates, Lt, 57
George, Lloyd (Prime Minister), 5
Gillespie, Robert (Maisie's husband), 137, 139, 143
Glenn, Lt, 57
Glover, George, 46, 48, 61-2
Gordon Highlanders, 22
Grier, Beth, 130-1
Guysborough, 101-102, 104

Haddington, 72-3
Hague Conventions, 36, 49
Haldane, Gen, 22
Handelsschule, 74, 76
Harvard University, 22, 125
Haubourdin, 33
Heidelberg, 4
Hendel, Charles, 62, 91, 95, 98, 132, 145
Hesepe Prison Camp, 51-60, 64-8, 115, 119, 142
Hetherington, Hector (Professor of Moral Philosophy Glasgow University, later its Principal), 124
Heusmann, Herr, 74-5
Hibben, John Grier (President of Princeton University), 46, 80, 90, 93, 97, 100-01, 103, 106, 110, 112, 125, 130-1, 141
Highland Light Infantry, 4, 38, 73
10/11th Battalion, 1, 14, 18, 24-5, 28-32, 45
13th Battalion, 7-8,
14th Battalion, 24-5, 41, 60
52nd Training Battalion, 10
Hindenburg Tunnel, 19
Hoare, Sir Samuel, 134
Hohnholz, Capt, Commandant, 51, 59-60, 65, 98-100
House of Commons, 74, 122-3, 134

Indian Civil Service, 137, 144
Ireland, 73
Islay, 3

Jacobus, Dr (a trustee of Princeton University) 138
John Lane publishers, 84-5

Johnson, RBC (chairman of Philosophy Princeton), 125
Jones, Capt, 57

Karney, Rev Arthur, 40, 55-8, 67, 72, 115, 137
Kant, Immanuel, 17-18, 48-9, 65
Keele University, 144
King, Alexander (Archie's uncle), 8
Kommandantur, 49, 64, 69
King George V, 6, 18,

Latta, Robert (Professor of Logic and Rhetoric, Glasgow), 110
La Grande Illusion (film directed by Jean Renoir), 59
Lavantie, 29-30
League of Nations, 73, 95, 115, 120-3, 126-7, 133-4, 140-1
Leven, 10, 61
Le Petit Mortier, 44
Le Touquet, 22, 40
Leipzig, 4, 63
Liebknecht, Karl, 72
Lille, 33, 53
Lindsay, Alexander, 108
Liverpool, 94
Ludendorff, Gen, 27
Lushai Hills Total Defence Scheme, 143
Luxemburg, Rosa, 72
Lys, the river, 1, 27-8, 36, 39, 43-4

MacAlister, Sir Donald (Principal of Glasgow University), 110-11, 116
Mackay, Harry, Maj, 10, 41, 43-5, 60-1, 76
Maclean, Capt, 3
McElroy, Miss (Head of Spence School), 107
McGill University, 101, 132
McGrigor, Sir Charles R, 36
McLauchlan, Lieut, 25, 44-5
McCosh, James (A President of Princeton), 5, 96-7
Manchester University, 61
Marburg University, 61
Marshall, Capt, 44,
Maryhill Barracks, 4, 73
Megantic (passenger liner), 94
Michels, Fräulein, 78-9, 86
Ministry of Information, 10, 17, 67, 74
Montreal, 42, 94, 109, 132

Mory, 20
Munro, Neil, 6

New York Times, 1, 46, 48, 61, 94, 96, 113
Nijmegen, 70
Northumberland Fusiliers, 68
Nouveau Monde, 27-9
Nova Scotia, 100, 138

Oppenheim, Baron, 86
Osman, Capt, 78, 89-90
Osnabrück, 66

Paris-Plage, 23
Peace Pledge Union, 145
Plato, 115, 119
Plumer, Gen, 27, 71
Portuguese Division, 2nd, 29
Princeton University, 1, 5-7, 22, 37, 46, 61-2, 72, 79-80, 82, 84-5, 90-1, 93, 120, 130, 132, 138, 140, 142, 145
Princeton Alumni Weekly, 131
Prior, Capt, 71
Proudfoot, William, 8

Rastatt Prison Camp, 35-40, 49, 51, 53, 115
Rathlin Island, 3
Red Cross, 22-3, 37, 45, 56
Rex Rheni (steam ship), 70
Rhine, 70, 72
Riehl, Professor Alois, 65
Robertson, Sir William (Commander of British Forces of the Rhine), 92
Rodin, Auguste, 25-6
Rogers, Capt, 63
Romeike, Henry, 46
Roosevelt, Franklin D (President of the United States), 131
Rotterdam, 70
Royal Air Force, 143, 147
Royal Army Medical Corps, 5, 57
Royal Artillery, 5
Royal Engineers, 5, 21, 42
Royal Society of Arts, 65

Sacramental Universe A (work by AA Bowman edited by JW Scott), 139, 144
Scots Observer (weekly paper), 120
Scott, John W (Professor of Logic and Moral Philosophy at University College Cardiff), 138

Senate (of the United States), 96
Siberian Expedition, 81-3, 85, 89
Sibilla, Fräulein, 79-80, 86, 93
Siegfried Line, 19
Sinn Féin, 73
Smith, Adam (Prof Moral Philosophy Glasgow University), 116
Smith, Norman Kemp, 5-7, 10-11, 17-18, 24, 31, 35, 37, 40, 44-8, 55, 63, 65, 67, 72-4, 76-7, 80, 82-5, 87-9, 91-5, 97-8, 101, 103-105, 108, 111-12, 118, 125, 127, 132, 138-40, 144
Sonnets from a Prison Camp (by AA Bowman), 84-5, 99, 104, 140
Spartacist, 72-3
Spence, Clara, 106-107
Spence School, 106-107
Spiers School, 4
Stewart, John (Mabel's brother), 19, 40, 42, 63-4, 69, 109
Stewart, Margaret (Norman's wife), 81-2
Stewart, Norman (Mabel's brother), 5, 81, 109
Stewart, Ronald (Mabel's brother), 5, 109
Stinnes, Hugo, 105-106
Storm Troops, 28, 30
Stuart Chair of Logic, 1,
Student Christian Movement, 137
Studies in the Philosophy of Religion (a work by AA Bowman edited by Norman Kemp Smith), 139, 141
Suffolk Regiment, 24

The Absurdity of Christianity (a short work by AA Bowman). 137, 145
The Beith Supplement and Advertiser, 133-4
The Flying Dutchman, 71
The Glasgow Herald, 43, 104, 119, 137
The Press and Journal, 118-19
The Scotsman, 133
The Times, 18, 137
Torrance, 137, 147-8
Traquair, Ramsay, (Professor of Architecture, McGill University, Montreal, 101
Treitsche, Henriech von, 4
Tuscania (passenger liner), 2-3

University College Ibadan, 144
University of California at Berkeley, 124-5, 138
University of California at Los Angeles, 108-109

University of Edinburgh, 93-4
University of Glasgow, 2, 17, 37, 74, 101, 103, 108, 110-11, 115-37, 139-40
University of Liverpool, 124

Vanuxem, 130-1, 138-9
War Office, 45-6, 72, 82, 85
Westphalia, 54

Whitehead, Alfred N (Professor of Philosophy at Harvard University), 125
Wilson, Woodrow (President of the United States), 2, 5, 89, 95-6, 120
Windygates, 10-13
Witherspoon, John (1st President of Princeton), 96
Workers' Educational Association, 115-20, 123